HOW I RAISED, FOLDED, BLUFFED, FLIRTED, CURSED, AND WON MILLIONS—
and You Can Too

HOW I RAISED, FOLDED, BLUFFED, FLIRTED, CURSED, AND WON MILLIONS—and You Can Too

ANNIE DUKE
with DAVID DIAMOND

Previously published as *Annie Duke*

A PLUME BOOK

PLUME
Published by Penguin Group
Penguin Group (USA) Inc., 375 Hudson Street, New York, New York 10014, U.S.A.
Penguin Group (Canada), 90 Eglinton Avenue East, Suite 700,
Toronto, Ontario, Canada M4P 2Y3 (a division of Pearson Penguin Canada Inc.)
Penguin Books Ltd., 80 Strand, London WC2R 0RL, England
Penguin Ireland, 25 St. Stephen's Green, Dublin 2, Ireland (a division of Penguin Books Ltd.)
Penguin Group (Australia), 250 Camberwell Road, Camberwell, Victoria 3124,
Australia (a division of Pearson Australia Group Pty. Ltd.)
Penguin Books India Pvt. Ltd., 11 Community Centre, Panchsheel Park,
New Delhi – 110 017, India
Penguin Books (NZ), cnr Airborne and Rosedale Roads, Albany, Auckland 1310,
New Zealand (a division of Pearson New Zealand Ltd.)
Penguin Books (South Africa) (Pty.) Ltd., 24 Sturdee Avenue, Rosebank,
Johannesburg 2196, South Africa

Penguin Books Ltd., Registered Offices: 80 Strand, London WC2R 0RL, England

Published by Plume, a member of Penguin Group (USA) Inc. Previously published in a Hudson Street Press edition under the title *Annie Duke.*

First Plume Printing, June 2006
10 9 8 7 6 5 4 3 2 1

Photo credits: 1–7. Courtesy of Richard Lederer and Simone van Egeren; 8. Courtesy of St. Paul's School archives; 9–16. Courtesy of Annie Duke; 17–18. Courtesy of Dale Parry; 19. Courtesy of Tom Sexton of Poker Masterpieces; 20–32. Courtesy of Eric D. Harkins and Image Masters PDI; 33. Courtesy of UltimateBet.com.

The Library of Congress has catalogued the Hudson Street Press edition as follows:

Duke, Annie, 1965–
Annie Duke : how I raised, folded, bluffed, flirted, cursed, and won millions at the world series of poker / Annie Duke ; with David Diamond.
p. cm.
ISBN 1-59463-012-7 (hc.)
ISBN 0-452-28648-4 (pbk.)
1. Duke, Annie, 1965– 2. Poker players—United States—Biography. 3. Women poker players—United States—Biography. I. Diamond, David. II. Title.
GV1250.2.D84A3 2005
794.412'092—dc22 2005012351

Printed in the United States of America
Original hardcover design by Eve L. Kirch

To my children Maud, Leo, Lucy, and Nelly.
I love you infinity.

So Here's the Deal on Poker

I'VE BEEN PLAYING POKER professionally for more than a decade, and not a day goes by when I play poker and don't learn from it, when I don't add something new to my game, when I don't see people differently. That's one of the amazing things about poker, one of the things that keeps people coming back for more—you never say, "Oh, I get it now," and move on to something else. Every time you sit down at a table, you're adding to your knowledge of the game. Even bad players offer insight, because there's no one I've ever played with who does *everything* wrong. Every bad player I know does one thing well, and figuring out which thing that is is an education in itself—and worth it. This is one game where you eventually use everything you've absorbed.

So for those of you who need a guide to the goings-on at a poker tournament, or who just want to bone up on the game, I've thrown together a primer, which you'll find at the back of the book. For novices, I've added such poker basics as the ranking of hands, betting fundamentals, and pokerspeak. I've also included the rules for Texas Hold 'em and Omaha Hi-Lo Split, the games played in the tournaments I describe. If you're a solid player, you can skip this section. But, then again, you might pick up something that will keep you from donking off your money. And I've included a Who's Who style guide to some of the players mentioned in this book—those I faced at the tables and those who were there to support me, and still are.

I've always thought that poker is a game that reveals itself as you play it. So that's how I've structured this book. I include tips that relate to what's happening in my tournament action—the strategy behind my moves and the theory behind that strategy.

I Never Set Out to Become a Professional Poker Player

I WAS SCHOOLED AT ST. PAUL'S, the fancy prep school where my father, a Ph.D. in linguistics, taught English; Columbia University, where I majored in both psychology and English literature; and the University of Pennsylvania, where, at the tender age of twenty-six, I was finishing my dissertation for a Ph.D. in psycholinguistics. I had already conducted years of research in language acquisition, written numerous academic papers, taught scores of students, and amassed an eight-page curriculum vitae that was impressive enough to earn me job talks—the precursor to a tenure-track position—at half a dozen top schools, including New York University.

The afternoon before I was scheduled to meet the academic committee at NYU, I drove my 1982 Honda from Philadelphia to New York, through the New Jersey vista of suburbs, salvage yards, and swamps. After dumping my car in a cheap overnight lot, I took the elevator up to my mother's two-bedroom apartment at 79th and Amsterdam.

It had been a few months since we'd seen each other and I remember thinking that she never seemed to change or age, with her dark hair still cropped below the ears and her unwavering fondness for earth tones. She was eager to see me—I was healthfully thin—and she was excited about the prospect of having me move back to New York. Proud of the future that was mine for the taking—an academic career that would ooze prominence and prosperity—my mom wanted to treat me to a little precelebration dinner. She ordered in Italian food, rigatoni with red sauce, from the Italian restaurant next to her apartment building, the place she ordered from every night.

Here, on a cold night in January 1992, is where my life in poker begins—and where the distinguished path that had been my academic career dead-ends.

We were sitting at my mom's kitchen table, talking, eating. Without any perceptible warning, somewhere within me a dam burst. A simple tin trash can stood below the table, teeming with loose-leaf pages of handwritten betting records.

I leaned over it and hurled.

Without sharing too many details, let's just say I did it again. And again. And again. I literally threw up all night, and in the morning I phoned NYU's psychology department and canceled my talk. Then I threw up again. The next day, my fiancé, Ben, drove me back to Philadelphia, where I spent the next two weeks in Graduate Hospital, unsuccessfully struggling to keep food in my system while a team of physicians labored to figure out what was wrong with me.

The answer was simple: I was afraid to grow up.

Steadied with drugs, I returned to the University of Pennsylvania campus. A few weeks after leaving the hospital, I stepped off the elevator, walked down a fluorescent-lighted hallway, and stood outside the classroom where I was to give a lecture on human cognition.

Suddenly, the dam broke again. How many people can honestly say they've experienced an out-and-out epiphany while puking? It struck me that I hadn't really chosen the life I was about to enter; I'd gotten there through inertia. When it came to facing the consequences of that inertia, I simply couldn't do it.

That's when I ran away. I fled to Montana, to marry a man I had never dated. And then, when money got tight and I felt beaten down by life in a leaky shack with minimal hot water and single-strand electricity, I got into my Honda and drove fifty-one frontier miles to the Crystal Lounge in Billings. I sat down at the poker table, among thick-fingered cowboys and boozing rednecks, slipped off my shoes, and tucked my bare feet under my butt—and as the dealer tossed me an ace-queen, I knew I was home.

This is where my life begins.

1

Sunday, May 9, 2004
11:55 A.M.

A CROWD HAS GATHERED, slowly, like a storm, inside Binion's Horseshoe Casino, for the 35th Annual World Series of Poker. Salesmen from the Great Plains; strip-mall real estate baronesses from the South; nail technicians and frat boys; physicians and Web designers. The overeducated and the underdressed hail from places as far and wide as Helsinki, Finland, and El Paso, Texas; Hendon, England, and Old Orchard Beach, Maine.

They've come to play in the $2,000 Buy-In Omaha Hi-Lo Split, which starts at noon. Or in the $1,000 Ladies Limit Hold 'em Event, scheduled to begin at two.

Players and spectators, alone and in pairs, mill about the pokerabilia vendors in the hallway and then, with their late-morning coffee, amble through the angled doorway, under the scripted words "Benny's Bullpen." It's fitting that the World Series of Poker takes place in a space named after the Vegas pioneer who was willing to host no-limit games, something that competing casino proprietors were too risk-averse to dare.

As noon approaches, they enter more purposefully, in packs of four or five. As the scrum of players and railbirds grows, so, too, do the noise and the anticipation. Dealers in black vests make their way to their tables. A waitress shifts the water bottles and soft drinks in the tray that hangs from her neck, then adjusts her tiny skirt. A team of masseurs and masseuses, all wearing identical red polo shirts, line a wall, ready to deliver back massages at the rate of a dollar per minute whenever a player gives the signal.

Players start taking their seats.

For eleven months of the year, Benny's Bullpen serves as the Bingo Room. And that feels about right. It's the size of your average catering hall or church basement, complete with dull paneling, acoustic-tile ceiling, and red carpeting that begs to be replaced. The room is windowless, and the air itself seems to date back to 1951, Binion's Horseshoe's virgin year.

Functional is how I'd describe this venue, chosen for the highest-stakes sporting event known to humanity. The only thing about it that says "Vegas" are the thousands of miniature, high-wattage klieg lights that beam down from the ceiling onto the green felt tops of forty-one kidney-shaped tables.

You spend a lot of time in this room—if you're lucky. It's divided into three distinct playing areas. There are twenty-six tables in a railed-off section to the right and rear of the room. Fourteen more tables are portioned off in the section to the left. Between these areas, with its own sense of importance, is the platform holding the final table. It's circled with TV camera stations and a row of chairs reserved for family and close friends. Tall bleachers sit on adjacent sides. When it isn't serving as a final table—that is, before the moment when only ten players are left to comprise a final table—this functions as the "featured" table. As with all tables, you end up here based on a random assignment. The dealer button position is selected with the draw of a card.

Primed as it is with lights and cameras, the featured table carries high odds that a camera will zoom in on you as you try to pressure an opponent to fold, or that you'll be the unfortunate object of the dreaded "death watch." That's when the cameraman hovers around, honing in on your expression of defeat and your measly stack of chips, as you have no choice but to move all-in. They're just waiting for you to lose.

Eventually, this becomes the final table, and the death watch notwithstanding, this is where you want to end up, with the nine other remaining players. Then eight. Then seven . . .

Just outside the metal rail, women sit at raised desks registering players for today's events—the $1,000 Ladies Tournament and the $2,000 Omaha Hi-Lo Split. Players line up. I stand behind a college-age fellow in a UTEP cap and T-shirt who glances nervously around the room, fingering the player's badge hanging from a lanyard around his neck, which could easily pass for a trade-show ID. To my right, I spot Mike Matusow chatting it up with anybody in his range, which, given the decibel level of his voice, extends pretty far. Over to my left I spot Brett Jungblut, large and laughing, a member of the young group of do-rag-wearing poker players famously dubbed The Crew on ESPN broadcasts. My friend Erik Seidel, who was a Wall Street success and world-class backgammon player before taking on Las Vegas and who has finished in the money thirty-one times (earning him a total of $2.36 million), sees me and greets me with a hug. The results from yesterday's event are posted on sheets of white paper that line the wall.

I step up to a desk to buy tournament chips, pulling $2,000 in folded-over hundred-dollar bills from my back pocket. In exchange, I'm handed $2,000 in chips, which I take to another desk—the registration desk—and use for the buy-in. I'm assigned to table seventeen, seat three, somewhere over to the right. I don't have a favorite table, but I do enjoy the few times I'm seated at the tables nearest the rail, so friends can hang nearby.

I know the drill. We play in sixty-minute rounds known as levels. We get a ten-minute break after every two rounds, and a sixty-minute dinner break following Level Six. In Level One, our blinds are $25 and $25, with betting limits of $25 for the initial bet and $50 for the second bet.

I sit down at the table and count my chips, then show the dealer my receipt. Next I take my iPod out of my purse, unwrapping the earphones and putting the device on the table. I leave my cell phone in my purse. At the table I see familiar faces. Men the Master. Perry Friedman. Toto Leonidas. Boston. The railbirds settle outside the play area. The ESPN crew of camera operators, sound-equipment folks, and clipboard-wielding producers take their places near the tables. Tournament Director Matt Savage, in a crisp black suit, grabs his microphone and introduces himself, welcoming spectators and participants and announcing the game we're about to play, almost as if we needed to make sure we have boarded the right flight. He says that 234 players will be competing in the $2,000 Omaha Hi-Lo Split. It's not surprising that only three of us are women, since two hours later 201 women will play in the Ladies Tournament. First prize in the Ladies Tournament is $58,530, with twenty-seven in the money. First prize in the Omaha Tournament will be $137,860, with twenty-seven in the money.

Then, pleasantly but matter-of-factly, Matt utters the four words that kick off every tournament, the five syllables that open up worlds of possibility:

"Shuffle up and deal."

♦ ♠ ♥ ♣

The World Series of Poker was born almost by accident. Not much more than a desert railroad town, the settlement of Las Vegas was incorporated in 1911, a few years after a drilling company discovered an underground water supply. Two decades later, the state of Nevada legalized gambling, which had been illegal between the years 1913 and 1931, setting the stage for a pair of modest casino hotels to be opened along U.S. 91 to Los Angeles, which would later become known as the Strip: the El Rancho Vegas, established in 1941, and the Last Frontier, which opened the following year. Even before those casinos were erected, Las Vegas had gained a reputation as an oasis of sin—during the 1930s it became the watering hole for workers on the Boulder Dam. But Las Vegas didn't really take off until 1946, when Bugsy Siegel erected the Flamingo. Gaudy and gangster-ridden, it launched Vegas as the world capital of frontier lavishness. Late that year, the Associated Press reported: "The town has been converted to an opulent playground."

Into this mix came Benny Binion, an outlaw entrepreneur who had built an illegal gambling empire in Texas before moving to Nevada, where he wouldn't have to spend so much time dodging the law. By 1949 Binion was the go-to host for high-stakes poker. When the famous gambler Nicholas "Nick the Greek" Dandolos told Binion he wanted to challenge the best player in the world in a no-limit marathon, Binion put out the word to Johnny Moss, a Texan and boyhood friend who was the best player he knew.

Binion, who had started his Vegas career as part owner of the Las Vegas Club, set the two players up at a table near the entrance to his new casino in downtown Las Vegas. In full public view Dandolos, fifty-seven, and Moss, forty-two, battled it out, playing every form of poker known to man. Sometimes, upward of three hundred spectators filled the hastily arranged chairs around their poker table. Sometimes, high rollers put up $10,000 to join the heads-up match, although none of them lasted very long.

The poker marathon endured for five months, reportedly with breaks only for sleep, about every four or five days. The stunt attracted hordes of gamblers and their dollars to Binion's casino. (This was a full two years before Frank Sinatra ever played Las Vegas.) Eventually, Moss defeated Dandolos, pocketing an estimated $2 million for his effort; adjusted for inflation, that would approach $100 million today. And when Dandolos finally turned over his losing hand, he rose from his chair, bowed slightly, and said: "Mr. Moss, I have to let you go."

It was the Dandolos-Moss marathon that inspired Binion to launch the World Series of Poker in the spring of 1970. In the ensuing years, Binion bought the El Dorado Hotel on Fremont Street in the heart of downtown and renamed it Binion's

Horseshoe, making it the first casino with carpeting. He also spent forty-two months in prison on tax-evasion charges.

In the spring of 1970, on campuses throughout the United States, students were reacting to the shooting deaths of four anti–Vietnam War protestors by National Guardsmen at Ohio's Kent State University. In Las Vegas, Elvis was riding a recent comeback to perform nightly at the International Hotel (now the Las Vegas Hilton)—taking breaks to fly to Nashville to record such songs as "Make the World Go Away" and "Funny, How Time Slips Away." Perry Como, too, was a headliner in Vegas in 1970, crooning "Love Is Spreading Over the World," while local legend Liberace leveraged his unfathomable celebrity to publish *Liberace Cooks!*, Polish-Italian recipes from his seven dining rooms. That year, the Las Vegas Drinking Water Pipeline was constructed to bring treated water from Lake Mead into Las Vegas, the population of which now approached 126,000. There was no such thing as tournament poker until Benny Binion invented the World Series in order to crown a champion, and also to lure railbirds who might also gamble to Binion's Horseshoe Casino, which a few years earlier had sprouted its trademark turquoise neon. For the first annual World Series of Poker, Binion assembled seven top players. In addition to Moss, they included a few others who were gaining national reputations as high-stakes players. Among them were Thomas "Amarillo Slim" Preston, the arrogant, outspoken Texas panhandle rancher who had once beaten Minnesota Fats at pool with a broom-handle cue; and Doyle "Texas Dolly" Brunson, *another* Texan, who has become one of poker's most enduring figures by winning nine WSOP bracelets.

There was something delightfully naïve about that first World Series. It was structured so that the seven players would compete among themselves and then *vote* for the best all-around player, who walked away with the title of World Champion and nothing else to enhance his bankroll. In 1970, twenty-one years after his victory in the famous heads-up match with Nick Dandolos, a now sixty-three-year-old Moss emerged the winner.

The following year, Binion altered the tournament to its current format: instead of *voting* for a winner, everybody plays until a single player rakes in all the chips. In 1971, Moss won again. And Binion established a cash prize: $30,000. When Amarillo Slim took the championship title from Moss in 1972, he donned his white Stetson and embarked on the talk-show circuit, an act that significantly raised his profile—and that of the World Series.

With each year that passed, Binion's little venture multiplied, in terms of both participants and cash prizes. He changed the structure so that the entire World Series didn't rest on a single event. Instead, throughout the course of a month, participants would compete in a series of smaller tournaments covering such games as Seven-Card Stud, Razz, Deuce-to-Seven, and Omaha Hi-Lo, requiring buy-ins ranging from $1,000 to $5,000. For each of these events—and now there are thirty-two of them—the top winners get a proportionate share of the prize pool, and the ultimate winner is also awarded a gold bracelet.

These events are followed by the main event, also known as the World Championship—that's the $10,000 Texas Hold 'em event that lasts five or more days and comes with the largest prize of any sporting event. More than the Kentucky Derby. More than Wimbledon. As we signed up for and played in the early tournaments, we couldn't have imagined that first place in the World Championship would yield a $5 million prize that, with twice the number of entrants, doubled the $2.5 million awarded in 2003. Unlike its namesake in baseball, the World Series of Poker truly is a world competition—hence the profusion of languages spoken and the diversity in apparel worn. That's an Arab seated next to a Jew. Retirees go heads-up with college sophomores. Physicians sit next to street toughs. In addition to being international, multicultural, and nondiscriminatory, the World Series of Poker is also astoundingly democratic from a skill perspective, with hobbyists who scrape together the cash for the buy-in playing at the same table as the pros.

Perhaps the biggest change in the World Series' thirty-five-year history was the introduction of satellite tournaments in the early 1980s. That's when Binion's started hosting low-buy-in games in which the winner earned not a cash prize but a seat in World Series events. Then the cyberspace era brought with it online poker, which began awarding the winners of Internet satellites seats in the World Series. Combined, both developments contributed to the boom in participants.

With the biggest stakes and highest prestige, the World Series of Poker is the pinnacle of poker achievement. It is simply the world's greatest card game. Everybody who plays poker for a living knows that Johnny Moss won the first World Series, and that Doyle Brunson won two. And that Johnny Chan won two back-to-back, and then came in second the following year.

Everybody who plays poker for a living knows that Stu Unger won two and descended into a world of cocaine, and then brought himself back—he got it together to win a third time, in 1999.

I came to Las Vegas a week ago to play in the 2004 World Series of Poker. By the time I arrived the series was into its tenth event; I bagged the first ten events because I wanted to spend time with my kids at home in Portland. With my extensive travel schedule, I don't feel I get to spend enough time with them. Just prior to coming to the series, I had to fly to London for less than thirty-six hours to present a trophy to the owner of the winning horse in the Guineas Festival (England's equivalent of the Preakness or Belmont Stakes). A few weeks before I had never even heard of the Guineas Festival; but this year, ultimatebet.com, the online poker site I work with, was a sponsor. So on my first trip to England, I combated jet lag, handed a bronze trophy to a sheik from Dubai, grinned for cameras, and shook hands. Then I flew to Vegas.

The flight path took us over the Arctic Circle, and then directly over Montana, the place I left behind when I discovered poker. I started playing because my then-husband, Ben, and I couldn't afford the $125-a-month mortgage on our four-hundred-square-foot love shack in Columbus, fifty-one miles west of Billings. I started playing because nothing else made me happy at the time, and because my brother, Howard, had become a poker pro and encouraged me to follow suit. I played because, in retrospect, it was the obvious choice for someone whose growing-up years revolved around family card games, and, maybe more importantly, around the lesson of winning at all costs.

A decade later I have four kids and live in a solid three-story home in a leafy Portland neighborhood. And I'm considered one of the best poker players in the world, despite the fact that I've not yet won a tournament in the World Series of Poker. I know the rap on me: despite the autograph seekers and television exposure, the lack of a World Series bracelet makes me something of a tournament also-ran, an embarrassing and painful reality. I lead in money winners for women. I have succeeded to the most final tables among women in World Series tournaments, and the most times in the money. But it still bothers me that I've never actually *won* a World Series tournament. It has all been heartbreaking seconds and thirds. In 1999, I had the $5,000 Limit Hold 'em event won with one card to come. I was the 6-to-1 favorite until the final card. A 5 came on the river to give my opponent a straight. Crushed, I ended up in second place.

And the 2004 World Series is turning out to be no different. Replaying the K-10 that caused me to lose all my remaining chips in yesterday's Limit Hold 'em Shoot-out, the seventeenth of thirty-three events in the monthlong series, makes me think of how hard I've been struggling with my mental game over the last few years, at a time when the stakes were getting higher than ever.

The astounding popularity of televised and online poker means millions of new eyes are focused on professional players like me. It also intensifies the pressure to succeed.

As poker's popularity surges, my own performance is tanking.

2

DEPENDING ON WHICH HISTORIAN you choose to believe, the game of poker may have been around in some form or another as early as ninth-century China. But there's no debating the fact that the year 2003 was the one in which it gained the greatest mass-market recognition. In the spring of that year, documentary filmmaker Steve Lipscomb launched the World Poker Tour on cable TV's Travel Channel, finally making poker accessible to a mass audience by introducing the lipstick camera—a gimmick from a British TV program—to U.S. television audiences. With a tiny camera implanted into the side of a poker table, for the first time viewers could peek at the two facedown "hole" cards that are dealt to each player at the start of a hand in Texas Hold 'em. Without knowing what cards players are holding, watching a poker competition would be about as thrilling as listening to a chess match on the radio. The lipstick camera changed that—and changed the game of poker forever.

The other phenomenon propelling poker to new heights

of popularity was the Internet. With a proliferation of online poker sites, now a multibillion-dollar business, a cash game was suddenly as accessible and convenient as a computer mouse and browser. According to PokerPulse, a Canadian company that keeps track of such statistics, in the early days of 2003, before poker hit television, online poker sites pulled in $300,000 in daily "rake," the small percentage of every hand played (capped online at $3) that the house or site gets as compensation for running the game. Eighteen months later that figure had jumped to $3.2 million a day. Every day, online players were wagering about $124 million in more than one hundred online poker rooms. And only 2 percent of the poker players in the world actually play online. By some estimates, there are as many as 60 million poker players in the United States, and that number seems to be growing.

One unexpected outcome of the vast amount of electronic play is that a new generation of poker aficionados was born and began perfecting skills far faster than was humanly possible in the analog world. In the 1990s, it would have taken you twenty years to achieve the level of experience that you can now get in a year from playing online. This fact became evident in the 2003 World Series of Poker when, in an upset that would have been unthinkable twelve months earlier, an Internet almost-amateur outlasted scores of professionals—including me—to win the final table of the main event. Chris Moneymaker, a twenty-seven-year-old accountant from Tennessee, had parlayed a $40 Texas Hold 'em poker tournament on the Internet into a seat in the World Series of Poker. To the astonishment of pros—and almost everybody else—he ended up at the final table, and ultimately won it all. Wearing bugeye sunglasses, he beamed as the tournament officials dumped $2.5 million—a mountain of 250 neatly bound packets of $10,000—onto the final table, as yellow-plumed showgirls and tournament officials posed behind him for photo ops.

Moneymaker's improbable win alone has brought poker to millions who would never have considered setting foot inside a brick-and-mortar casino. Poker seems to have replaced video games and garage bands as the number-one after-school activity among high school boys. Poker rooms, in the twenty-two states where they're legal (and elsewhere, in Indian casinos) are packed to capacity—put your name on the list for a seat at a Texas Hold 'em table at the mammoth San Pablo Casino in San Pablo, California, and you might just find yourself waiting on the sidelines for an hour. A Wichita company has created the Amateur Poker League, whose thousands of members play in 150 bars and other locations in Kansas, Missouri, Texas, Illinois, and California. And, while long a tradition in certain circles, poker night has expanded in some interesting and unanticipated directions—I recently met someone whose Friday-night religious ritual has morphed into Poker Shabbat.

Poker has endured for centuries in large part because it challenges on so many levels. It requires you to make split-second statistical calculations at the same time you're reading your opponents for psychological and physical clues about what cards they're holding or what moves they're likely to make. Poker requires you to be an actor, deliberately misleading others about your intentions, hiding your excitement or disappointment in a hand. It can be frustrating, exhilarating, humiliating, even brutal. But it's rarely uninteresting. When it *is*, that means it's time to move up to more challenging players, and the possibility of earning more cash.

People often ask me what it is that I love about the game. When I pull it all together and play a hand as it should be played—when I get lucky with my cards—I feel the surge that I imagine quarterbacks feel when they throw a touchdown pass, or that writers feel when they nail a perfect paragraph, or that IRS agents feel when they nab a cheat.

I feel invincible.

♦ ♠ ♥ ♣

So, as poker skyrocketed in popularity and my own performance became lackluster, my responsibilities at home multiplied. I gave birth to four children over a period of eight years, while trying to play in enough events to support my growing family *and* perfect the nuances of my skills in a game that, with the sudden infusion of millions of Moneymaker wannabes, was becoming more difficult.

I took breaks from poker after each of my children was born. And, like working moms in more traditional professions, I tried my best to balance the conflicting demands of family and career—missing important tournaments to dye Easter eggs with my kids or to attend school conferences or birthday parties. My play steadily improved, but when I was pregnant with Nelly (my fourth), I found myself under a lot of stress and wasn't playing as well as I could.

Like everything else in life, poker is in a constant state of change, with new players coming and going, new games gaining popularity, regular opponents honing new skills just when you thought you could predict their every move and run over them with ease. So your poker strategy must be flexible enough to adapt. You need to continually reassess what works and what doesn't—and adjust accordingly.

So after Nelly was born I took a break from tournament poker to retool my game. I needed to master the new landscape, which was becoming defined by the influx of Internet players, who were relatively inexperienced but frankly more aggressive than the traditional non-Internet professional. This meant trusting my instincts more when it came to playing a new opponent, understanding the new style of play and how it applied to the players. Which were callers? Which were folders? Which players were intimidated by me? And which players just wanted to beat me because of who I am?

Reworking the game and getting my timing down was crucial.

In the old days, you played against the sixty or so other best players in the world, and hyperaggression didn't work well against them. Great players are better readers, and they're going to play against you.

These days, you're playing against fields of six hundred relatively inexperienced players, who might buckle under pressure—or who just might be overly aggressive to prove their acumen. You're playing against six hundred completely unknown quantities. So sometimes hyperaggression works—you do a lot more rebluffing, you raise a higher percentage of the hands. You put a lot of chips at risk. You assume control and take over the table. But sometimes sitting back and trapping the hyperaggressor is the way to go. You have to retool your game for all sorts of new players. I succeeded in retooling my game, only to get hit with a sledgehammer; my marriage imploded. In November 2003, Ben and I called it quits. It was a long time coming. With four kids, and me being the primary breadwinner, it was now more important than ever that I succeed.

I was having difficulty putting my divorce out of my mind. Nevertheless, I registered for the $2,500 Buy-In Limit Hold 'em event in the Bellagio Five-Star World Poker Classic/WPT Championship, which was held on Sunday, April 4, 2004. Most tournaments begin at noon and last all day, until all but nine players have been knocked out. Those players comprise the final table, and they resume play at two or three p.m. the following afternoon.

I was hopeful, but honestly, I had been so stung by previous poor performances that I actually booked an eight o'clock flight back to Portland for the following morning. I just didn't think I would make it to the final table. But I did.

At my first table I faced such tough opponents as Todd Brunson, who plays in some of the biggest cash games in the world; David Chiu, who's won three World Series of Poker bracelets; and Allen Cunningham, who is a two-time WSOP tournament winner. Very early on, the combination of betting the required blinds and losing hands knocked me down from my $5,000 in starting chips to a mere $900. I lucked out when I tripled up my chips with a pair of aces, and by dinner I had amassed $47,000, more than twice the average. I canceled my flight.

At the final table the next day, I became chip leader when I semi-bluffed and landed a flush. Ultimately I went heads-up against Daniel Quach, a quiet player from Monrovia, California, who dresses in the standard poker player uniform of jeans and a T-shirt and who was easy to read: he plays his weak hands fast and his strong hands slow. I had amazing luck—and the rush of my life. Four times in a row when I was in the big blind, Daniel raised and I had A-Q. I reraised each time, and each time I flopped top pair. Ultimately, I was holding A-10 (diamonds). He raised. I reraised. He called. The board came A-Q-10, giving me two pair. I bet. He called. The turn was a 7 and he went all-in. He had 10-7 for bottom two pair. My top two pair—aces and queens—held up, and I won the tournament. Howard had been standing behind me for the entire final table. I jumped into his arms.

Then I collected my $157,000.

I was back.

Or so I thought.

By the time the World Series got under way a few weeks later, in late April 2004, I felt confident in my game. But on Tuesday morning, May 4, a few hours before the $5,000 No-Limit Hold 'em event was to begin, I phoned Ben to work out some details of our impending divorce. There was no way to postpone the call; the World Series of Poker stretches for six weeks, and the only time to talk to him is in the mornings, before tournaments begin. Our discussion degenerated into a bitter argument, and I hung up the phone feeling emotionally immobilized.

I couldn't sit at the table. I couldn't concentrate on the game.

Professional poker players tend not to be superstitious (as

the old joke goes, it's bad luck to be superstitious!), but there are a few scenarios that commonly go hand in hand with losing streaks. One is called the "House Curse": you buy a new house, you've made a big financial commitment that adds a significant layer of stress to your game, you start to lose, and it's one big vicious circle.

I was wrestling with what might just as easily have been called the Divorce Curse. I was emotionally raw. I was rattled from my conversation with Ben. I had no patience, and my play suffered. When I found myself increasingly stressed to pay attention, I just kept thinking—particularly when I got short-stacked—that I'd have to somehow drag the play out for hours until I got a rush of good cards. And without the ability to concentrate, that wasn't going to occur. "Tilted" is the poker term for getting emotionally thrown off your game, and I was well on my way.

But I caught it in time.

It happened that on May 6 I was in the $2,000 Buy-In Limit Hold 'em event of the World Series, listening to the Violent Femmes on my iPod and losing hands I didn't need to lose. I think that most experienced pros, especially the more mathematically minded ones, tend to be realistic about assessing winning and losing streaks. I focused in on what, in particular, was wrong with the situation at hand.

I was struggling with the miserable, trapped feeling that I couldn't just get up and leave. It's a feeling I've had for years in other settings—classes, movies, dinner. It was distracting, to say the least. And it was making me unbearably impatient.

In poker, as in life, you've got to know what you need in

order to succeed. Sometimes, it's obvious. New players can't hope to win at poker without understanding the statistical odds of a hand or the importance of betting position to your play. For those beginners, it makes sense to systematically identify the lapses in skills and knowledge, and then just as systematically go about fixing them. But often, it's not easy to pinpoint what it is that's stalling you. It might not be obvious that you're losing hands because you've stopped paying attention to the patterns in your opponents' play, that what you might need is to take a brisk walk around the block to get out of your own way, or to just call it a night. It might not be obvious that you're failing to maximize your win because you're playing too tight for that particular situation. Maybe you're playing tight because you lost too much money in last week's game to players who were far better than you. So you're afraid of repeating last week's experience, even though you're now playing with less-skilled players and can *afford* to play a looser game.

If you're not satisfied with your game, you need to continually think about what you can do on your own to improve it.

That's what I did. I figured that my best bet was to play in a cash game, where I could leave at any time, just to see how long I could sit there. So at about two p.m., I lost all my chips in the Limit Hold 'em event. I left the table and made my way out of Binion's Horseshoe tournament room, past the folks peddling World Series of Poker memorabilia and others hawking poker books, past the nearly empty buffet, down the escalator to the threadbare glamour of the Horseshoe Casino, and out to the valet parking deck. I waited beneath an advertisement for Belvedere Vodka, a highly stylized drawing of my brother Howard and me that was part of a series of ads that descended upon Las Vegas during the World Series, appearing everywhere from magazines to taxicabs. When the rental car arrived, I drove in the oppressive sunshine from the funk of downtown Vegas to the shopping-mall opulence of the Strip. I was in search of a cash game.

The Bellagio's high-limit poker room sits about two feet above the rest of the casino floor. The walls feature Italianate tapestries depicting the regal life of bygone centuries in the vicinity of Bellagio, Italy. Above them TV monitors broadcast basketball, hockey, golf, tennis—whatever's in season. There, on chairs upholstered in sickly green, maroon, and white stripes, in the relative ease of a cash game, I came back.

Table number one, in the farthest corner, is where the highest-limit games take place. It is, unquestionably, the biggest game in town, if not the world. The stakes usually range from $1,000-$2,000 to $1,500-$3,000—in Limit Hold 'em, the third and fourth rounds of betting are twice that of the first two rounds. The minimum required to sit at the table is $20,000, but most people bring much more than that. Single pots can reach $50,000. On any given night, you might find the likes of Doyle Brunson or Johnny Chan or a random billionaire from Texas itching to go heads-up with the best pros. (Bill Gates, that billionaire from Washington State, plays at the Bellagio, too. But he shies away from high-limit games. In fact, he sticks with $3-$6 games. And trust me, he's smart to do that. The best players in the world wouldn't pit their programming skills against his.)

I chose to play table number two instead, a $400-$800

mixed game, where I was able to sit for eight hours, trying to prove to myself that I could concentrate for an extended period of time. And I did, winning $18,000 from a succession of assorted high-rolling players. I had demonstrated to myself that I could transcend the deep, emotional feelings I was having about my divorce—at least long enough to do my job effectively. I had rediscovered my patience.

3

Sunday, May 9, 2004
2:00 P.M.

MEN THE MASTER is playing way too fast. Which is great.

I love having someone on my right who is raising too much—then I can punish them by isolating them when I have good hands. Men is not alone in his looseness; in Omaha, you typically play 20 percent of your hands. But the people at this table are well above that, sometimes playing as many as 50 percent. In seat number one is my friend Perry Friedman, who wrote a program for the game Roshambo. In seat number two is the legendary Men "the Master" Nguyen. In three is me. In seat number four, to my immediate left, is Boston (a.k.a. Alan Dvorkis, the great college basketball handicapper, looking his usual aggravated self to be in the room—it's one of the things about him that I find most endearing).

I don't know any of the other six players, but they're all men. One looks almost buried in a thick brown sweat suit and a leather jacket, not quite the attire for the Las Vegas heat, but just the thing to wear in an overly air-conditioned casino. Another has spent longer than necessary cleaning his brand-name shades at the table, spitting on one side of the lens, polishing it with his silk Tommy Bahama shirt, holding it up to the light to look for smudges, then spitting again—four times each—on the lenses. Another player, a buffed, goateed kid in his twenties wearing a red Budweiser T-shirt, stares off into space, probably listening to Franz Ferdinand on his MP3 player. He's rockin' to the music, literally, tapping out the tune on the table with his fingertips.

No, wait, he stopped. Okay, now he's doing it again.

Without being obvious, I do what I always do at the start of poker games. I watch and listen, as a way of getting a handle on each of my opponents. It's not as if there are standard psychological profiles, but I assign one to each player. In the early moments at the table, I just make a guess at what a player's personality is like, then try to figure out how that personality would act under certain conditions. I consider the frustration factor. If someone strikes me as easily frustrated, he's probably not a risk taker. In which case frustration is likely to cause him to bluff. Does somebody get emotionally unhinged easily? Are they aggressive in conversation? Or are they sitting quietly? (If they're aggressive in conversation, I certainly know that they're much more likely to be bluffing than anyone else at the table. I stop to consider whether they're being aggressive toward me in particular. A lot of times people who aren't necessarily aggressive toward other people will be aggressive toward me because I'm a woman.)

Do they look nervous about the money? Are they recounting their chips, stacking them very neatly, maybe even by denomination? The more meticulous and methodical, the more easily bluffed.

Before play begins, I try to get a baseline on players' blink rates. It's common knowledge that people tend to blink more when they're lying. So before the cards arrive, I watch their eyes. And their mouths, too—there are hundreds of possible tells in the expression of the human mouth.

The genius of Omaha 8-or-Better is that because you get dealt four cards, a creative mind can conjure a lot of good combinations of cards to play because people feel like it doubles the possibilities over Hold 'em. So what happens? Folks tend to play Omaha 8-or-Better much looser than Hold 'em, assuming they'll make one of those combinations. But the reality is that Omaha should be played slightly tighter than Hold 'em, for two reasons. First, there's the nagging fact that you're often giving up half the pot, since it's split between the low and the high hand, when somebody has a low. So the pot's never laying you the same kind of price to hit your nut hand as it would in Hold 'em. Second, there are a lot more cards out against

Always think ahead. Poker is about making decisions amid uncertainty.

Poker is like chess—if you blacked out one-quarter of the board. You make a decision knowing there are fingers of consequences fanning out, and you have to keep track of all the possibilities. While trying to decide the primary line of play, you also have to contemplate secondary and tertiary lines of play. You may have the whole decision tree, but you lack access to all the information needed to make those decisions.

you. So if you think about it, in Hold 'em, if it's you and two other people, there are only four cards out against you. In Omaha, there are eight. With double the number of cards out against you, the quality of your hand has to increase to compensate for the potential that those cards will produce a hand that's better than yours.

But such loose playing by my opponents is allowing me to boost my chip stack, bit by bit. We started with $2,000 in chips, and I've increased that to about $4,000.

At the $100-$200 limit, Men raises in first position, typical of his loose and aggressive style of play.

I reraise him, holding A-2-5-10 (double suited). I have a strong hi-lo hand, so I'm reraising for value. But I'm also reraising as a move intended to eliminate other players and isolate Men, who is playing every hand. The combination of factors—my good cards and his loose playing—means that I have a solid chance of raking a big pot from him if we go heads-up.

Everyone folds to Perry, who was in the small blind. He calls.

Men raises again.

I call.

Perry calls.

The board comes 4-6-8. Men calls all-in.

I raise. Perry calls.

Ultimately, when we turn over the cards, Perry and I split the pot. I get the low side and Perry, with A-8-8-J, wins the high side with three 8s. Men's hand was A-5-6-10.

With a hand like that you normally don't raise in first position. It's not a good enough hand to put the first bet in. It's great that Men is playing too loose. I wish I knew how to say "thank you" in Vietnamese.

Such wins notwithstanding, I'm not doing spectacularly well, but I'm doing okay with what I have. I know I have to be patient until the decent cards materialize.

Soon, it's time for the tournament organizers to condense tables to adjust for players who got knocked out early. Our table breaks up, and we're each assigned to another. I move to table number 11—within easy range of the Ladies Tournament. ESPN swings a camera over to ask me why I'm playing in this event. For days, they've been trying to convince me to play in the Ladies Tournament instead of the Omaha Hi-Lo Split, which is taking place at the same time. Their reason? They're televising the Ladies Tournament, not the Omaha. Kathy Liebert and Cyndy Violette are there.

Understand the importance of position.

Position is important because you get to reduce the amount of uncertainty, which increases the likelihood that you'll make good decisions. In Texas Hold 'em, your betting position is a critical factor in how you play your hand. Late position—being one of the last to bet—is superior since you have the knowledge of what your opponents have done before you.

Good players tend to play more hands in late position. The opposite is true for early position. You're disadvantaged by the fact that there are so many players behind you and you don't know what they'll do. Avoid playing marginal hands in early position.

Jennifer Harman and I—clearly two of the top women players in the world—are not. In Jennifer's case, it's because she's seriously ill. In my case, it's simply a business decision: Omaha is a great game for me. With Omaha, there's a bigger gap between me and my opponents than there is in Limit Hold 'em. And look at the numbers. There are 201 women competing in the Ladies event. With a buy-in of $1,000, that puts the total prize pool at $201,000; first prize will net around $58,000. Whereas 234 players paid $2,000 each to compete in the Omaha tournament; that means the winner will walk off with something approaching $138,600. That's nearly three times what could be earned in the Ladies event. And in a field that large, there are always a lot of big dogs to the good players. Clearly, more money is to be won in Omaha.

"This is where the money is," I tell ESPN. "This is what I do for a living."

My second table really sucks; the players—like Chris "Jesus" Ferguson, who won the 2000 World Series of Poker Championship;

Forget the suits.

Don't get carried away with suited cards. All suitedness does is take a marginal hand and turn it into a playable hand. A very, very good hand is improved about 2 percent by being suited. A very, very bad hand—say 7-2 offsuit—would be improved by about 12 percent, but it's still 7 high, and you're probably not going to make the flush. Even if you do, it's only a 7-high flush.

Allen Cunningham, the young and young-looking winner of two WSOP bracelets; and Toto Leonidas, winner of the 2003 World Series of Poker $1,500 Seven-Card Stud event—pose some stiff competition. As with my previous table, there is someone at this one, I don't know who he is, who plays a lot more hands than most people would play. He is a friendly, portly Southerner sporting a World Series of Poker bracelet. But unlike Men, who had been overplaying and losing, this guy is hitting—and scooping every pot. Unlike my other table, where I was hitting good, steady cards, my cards here are bleak, and with someone loose on my right, I can't bluff. I'm blinding my money off.

So at our table Perry raises in front of him. And this guy (who, as it turns out, will have something on the order of 2-2-7-Q) calls. That's a hand that you'd never play. But for whatever reason, he plays it and wins. That's the way the cards are hitting for him. Mr. Confederacy is constructing skyscrapers from his chips.

For me, it's the opposite. I'm starting to get card dead. My stack has been whittled down to $4,000 and we are approaching the $200-$400 level. I drink a Diet Coke, then order another.

Hand after hand, my cards suck. My hand is A-3-J-9, which, at this point, because my hands have been so bad, actually starts looking really good to me. But I resist the urge to play and that turns out to be the right decision. I had three cards in my hand higher than 9, and two of the lowest cards you could have. But someone reraised, meaning there was a likelihood I would be scooped with an opponent holding A-2. That one hand would have ended my tournament right there.

Many players would have given in and played that hand. It had high possibilities. It had low possibilities. But against the reraise, it was likely that I would be sucking wind. And it turned out I was right.

Like singles beer-goggling at a bar after last call, just because you haven't had any cards for a long stretch of time doesn't mean that you should fall for a bad hand that's starting to look good to you. This is easier said than done, but when you're card dead, it's a mental battle not to play a hand that you think has possibilities. There are a couple of good reasons why most pros can endure a streak of bad cards while less experienced players might freak. First, as pros, we've learned patience, and can better discern a good hand from a bad one. I like to think of it as creating your luck—you put yourself in the most advantageous position for when the right cards arrive.

I've heard people say Gus Hansen, three-time World Poker Tour champ, is very lucky. But the fact is, he's prepared himself for those lucky moments. In my case, at this point, I'm just trying to stay in the tournament, to play well enough to survive the card drought so that I can reap the rewards when the cards do eventually come my way.

Luckily, my patience pays off, and I win most of the hands that I choose to play. I'm getting just enough good starting cards that I'm able to raise and win enough to keep up with the $75-$150 blinds.

You should never play a hand like 2-2-7-Q in Omaha.

Any hand with an ace and a small card can beat you on the low. And if you flop a set for the high, you're going to get beat by a higher set. The hand literally has no potential.

But it's not easy. Because I'm not playing many hands, my stack of chips is shrinking closer to the felt, thanks to the blinds and the betting limits of $150-$300. The blinds and limits increase every hour. As people get eliminated, other players collect more chips. So in order to make the limit commensurate with the consolidated chip stacks, they keep raising the blinds (if they didn't, the tournament would never end). They raise the blinds to create action, and so that the average player always has something like thirty big bets in his or her stack.

I have $1,125 in chips. When the limits go up in the next round, I will only have enough for one bet. I get moved to yet another table.

I pick up my cards and see A-2-Q-9. I raise before the flop and get called by Toto Leonidas.

The flop is 3-4-9.

I bet on the flop and Toto calls.

I'm down to $675 in chips.

The turn is an 8.

I bet on the turn and he calls.

That puts me down to $375 in chips. This is okay. I've never come in first or second in a tournament where I wasn't at some point close to the felt. At times it was in the beginning of a tournament; other times, it was at the final table. I've been down to a single bet and survived to win a tournament.

I can still make it.

The dealer flips over a queen for the river. But the river bet leaves me with exactly $75 in chips. A player I know who was a doctor for the Centers for Disease Control says, "Remember that you only had seventy-five dollars when you win this."

Toto calls.

It's a terrific moment for me. With $75 in chips, I won't last more than a few more minutes in this game unless I win this hand. But I have the nut low and top two pair, so I'm likely to win the pot. I fold my arms and readjust my legs, which are tucked under me on the chair, and turn over my hand.

I scoop it. Perfect.

A massive video display high up on a wall in Benny's Bullpen keeps us abreast of tournament level, number of players remaining, and big and small blinds. And, most important, the hours, minutes, and seconds to our next break. As soon as the digital clock indicates it's time to stop playing, we hear the welcome sound of the buzzer and a tournament official announcing the ten-minute break.

I dart out past the railbirds to the bench down the hall from the Bullpen. That bench is my home away from home, the place where I spend most of my time during the quick breaks. It sits opposite a collection of candy machines. Everybody passes by on their way to the elevators that take you down to the casino and out onto the "Fremont Street Experience" or the alleyway that runs along the side of Binion's Horseshoe. A parade of players racing to grab a quick cigarette rushes by, recalling details of hands won or lost: "queens full

Pay attention to how fast or slow people play particular hands.

It can help you predict what they're holding in future hands. Even if you're not playing a hand, you can watch for patterns in others' play.

of tens . . ."; "the asshole reraised me!"; "she moves all-in on the turn . . ."; "I'm such a donkey. Donkey. Donkey. Donkey."

Out on the bench, the pent-up emotions from the previous two hours of play spew forth in record time. Friends stop by, asking my opinion about a specific hand they played, or for advice about playing against a particular opponent. It really is something, the way the best players in the world, folks who've taken millions of dollars from other players at the poker table, will exit a tournament filled with self-doubt. One minute you're at a table, trying your best to put pressure on a grizzly player, acting tough and pulling every possible trick from your arsenal to convince the person to fold, while he's trying his best to stare you down or use other means of intimidation to get *you* to fold. The next minute you're sitting out on the bench trying not to break down over the fact that you misread an opponent's facial tic.

My friend Robert Williamson III, a brilliant player from Texas who assumes the I'm-just-an-ol'-country-boy persona to disarm opponents, walks by, asking if I have a big chip stack.

"Haven't donked off all of my money yet but I'm getting close," I say.

Ten minutes is not a lot of time, considering that you might just have to hit the ladies' room, and you have to check your voice mail. Sometimes it's hard to shift gears in that tiny window of time, especially when it comes to my kids. Every parent knows it's a constant tug-of-war. On the one hand, you want to check in with your kids, who are at your brother's house with their nanny and their cousin and a few extra youngsters who have dropped by. You want to know if they've spent the previous three hours without budging from their places in front of the TV screen, or if they've done something preferable, like swimming in the backyard pool. But you also don't know if you can go there right now. A quick call to check up on them might lead to a sibling squabble. Do you really want to be trying to figure out who scratched whom first in the three and a half minutes you've got to make it back to your table? Of course, it would be nice to phone up and hear Leo say, in his tender six-year-old voice, "Mom, I'm so proud of your accomplishments."

It would be all I'd need in the world. That and Diet Coke.

4

UNLIKE THE WAY RICHARD WILLIAMS intentionally created two tennis prodigies in his daughters Venus and Serena, my parents were unwitting in their nurturing of a pair of poker champs. But in retrospect, it's not all that surprising, considering that they met at Harvard's Graduate School of Education over a deck of cards, when my dad's bridge group needed a fourth player just as my mom happened to walk by.

My parents moved to Concord, New Hampshire, in 1961, when my dad signed on with what would become his first and only employer: St. Paul's School. Fresh from grad school, my father arrived on the campus with his young bride—my mom, Rhoda Ann, who went by Deedy—straight from their honeymoon-from-hell in Montauk, New York. (My father got lost driving from the nuptials at my mom's mother's house in Connecticut to the Plaza Hotel, where they were to spend their wedding night. They ended up in Harlem, mid–racial riot, where my father rolled down the window to ask for directions. They missed the performance of *No Strings Attached* they had tickets for and, after dinner at the Oak Room, my mom went upstairs to the room to throw up, the result of bad oysters. The next day, out on Montauk, there were problems with the house they intended to occupy for the week, so they stayed in a cheesy motel. Then a hurricane blew in. . . .)

After considering careers in medicine and law, Dad had decided he wanted to teach English, wanted to make a positive difference in the lives of young men—and it was all young men back then. Because St. Paul's refused to hire both members of a married couple, Mom, also certified to teach English, took a job at Concord High School. Like many women of her generation, Mom got started early on producing a family: my brother, Howard, was born in 1963. My dad had grown up in West Philadelphia and my mom in Winnetka, Illinois, and Darien, Connecticut, and there they were, hunkered down in postcardesque Concord, New Hampshire.

Like most of New England, the 40,000-population city of Concord is obsessed with its history. Located along the banks of the Merrimack River, the land had been home to Native Americans—the Penacook—for thousands of years by 1725, when a group of settlers from Massachusetts arrived, seeking better soil for farming and a river on which to transport goods. Local citizens served as rangers and scouts during the French and Indian War of 1754–1763. An assemblage of Shakers formed a settlement a few miles north of town in 1790. And Concord's more-or-less central location in the state made it a natural choice for New Hampshire's capital in the decades after the American Revolution. The gilt-domed statehouse that remains the focal point of downtown was erected in 1819.

Even today, Concord feels less like a bona fide city than like an American small town that happens to have a state capitol where a department store would typically be located. Once a center for the manufacture of stagecoaches, the community's long-shuttered factories produced the famous Concord Coach, "the coach that won the American West." Also long-shuttered are the textile mills that ringed the town. Today many of its residents work for the state government, but Concord has produced a few famous citizens: Franklin Pierce, America's fourteenth president (a one-termer); Mary Baker Eddy, founder of the Christian Science movement; Christa McAuliffe, the teacher who died aboard the space shuttle *Challenger*; and me, the first Lamaze baby born there.

Located on more than 2,000 wooded and ponded—*I know, Dad, it's not a word*—acres west of Concord's downtown, St. Paul's had, since its inception in 1856, built a deserved reputation as an academic training ground for the sons of America's WASP elite. Strongly Episcopalian in nature, populated by the heirs to America's commercial and industrial dynasties, the school strove to provide its students with both the religious and academic foundations that would enable them to honorably pursue their destinies.

In order to picture this place, imagine centuries-old gothic structures of stone and brick. (The "new" chapel was dedicated in 1888—that's the *new* one). With its leaded glass windows, aged red maples, and brick walkways set several feet back from the gently winding roadways, the school has worked hard at preserving a timeless quality. A single example pretty much says it all: the little alcoves in the road where cars are to be parked bear nothing as crass as white lines delineating spaces for vehicles. Adding to this otherworldliness, the school adheres to the British system of describing grade levels. In almost every other school in America—both public and private—twelfth-graders are referred to as twelfth-graders or seniors. At St. Paul's they're called "Sixth Formers." Here's a telling excerpt from *A Brief History of St. Paul's School*, by August Heckscher: "It is a community inextricably linked with the contemporary world and with the surrounding countryside; yet it stands somewhat apart, not quite of its own time in its conscious search for excellence, its adherence to long-ingrained ideals of learning and work, and its hope (like most hopes not always fulfilled!) of achieving a perfected communal existence."

In the entire English language, I'd say the words "perfected communal existence" probably would be the last three I would choose to describe the St. Paul's school where my father worked and where, as a faculty family, we lived like aliens among the privileged. For starters, my parents were not wealthy. Many of my father's faculty colleagues were themselves St. Paul's alumni. Like the children they taught, coached, and, as dorm masters, tucked in to bed, those faculty members oozed a sense of entitlement. For Christmas, they jetted off to the Caribbean. In summers, they retreated to their vacation homes on Nantucket. My father? The moment classes ended, he picked up a spatula and flipped burgers at the Howdy Beef & Burger in Concord.

In addition to the wealth factor, there was another massive cultural distinction. Despite my mom's Connecticut white-bread heritage, my father was undeniably Jewish. Neither of his parents had finished high school. He was the sole Jewish department head at one of the preppiest of preppy boarding schools in New England. To make matters worse, my parents were politically liberal in a sea of conservatism.

This was the environment in which my father chose to live and raise his family in the early 1960s. He considered teaching to be a noble profession, and was eager to expose the children of privilege to a liberal point of view. Ever the optimist, he relished it. Teaching kids grammar during the day. Coaching football and tennis in the afternoon. Working down in the dorm basement with the debate team or student newspaper in the early evening. Putting the kids—other people's kids—to bed at night. On weekends, he played tennis in local leagues or bridge with other faculty members. A workaholic by any standard, he pursued a Ph.D. at the University of New Hampshire and started writing entertaining books about the English language, such as *Anguished English* and *Fractured English.* While Mom also played bridge and joined my father in campus theater performances, she wasn't as enthralled by life at St. Paul's. An educated woman with an extremely quick mind, she harbored visions of becoming a professional actress. She hated the drudgery of housework. Worse, she hated the restrictions of life on a teacher's salary.

But when she got hold of a deck of cards, there was no holding her back, particularly if she was playing oh hell or gin or spoons. One of the most enduring legends from our family involves a game of spoons played in our kitchen sometime in the early summer of 1965. You know spoons? It's one of those frivolous games designed to get people to squeal in delight and draw blood. In addition to a deck of cards, there are spoons on the table—one fewer spoon than there are players. You're dealt four cards, and the remaining cards are kept facedown in a stack near the dealer. You take your turn picking up a card from the deck and adding it to your hand, then you pass along one card to the person to your left. You always have four cards in your hand. When someone gets four of a kind, they're supposed to pick up a spoon so that nobody notices. But when people notice one is gone, they go for the remaining spoons. Since someone will be left out in grabbing a spoon—and this is a fast-action game—people usually fight over them. I've got a tiny scar along the side of my right thumb from such an altercation when I was about seven years old. But back in 1965, my parents were going heads-up in a spoons match in the blue-tiled kitchen of our home and, of course, they got into a tussle. With neither parent willing to concede, my father—who was six feet one and weighed 190 pounds—literally dragged my mom across the kitchen floor.

She wouldn't let go. And she was seven months pregnant with me.

That drive to win at all costs—and that stubbornness—was passed down through the genes. I'm told that when I was two years old my mother pushed me along as I steadfastly refused to walk somewhere, and I turned and announced, *"You don't push people!"* When she grabbed me by the shoulder in a dime store when I was around three years old, I shouted, *"You're strangling my arm!"* Early on, my father was concerned that I might be mentally challenged—"retarded" was the word then—

because I had no interest in playing with toys or dolls. I only liked people.

When I was eight I discovered gymnastics. I was actually building the skills to become a competitive gymnast. Supportive of my passion, my parents spent countless hours shuttling me to events throughout greater Concord. Then, suddenly, I developed a horrible fear of going backward—of doing something where I couldn't see that my hands were going to land safely. Ironically, the forward moves are rated as being more difficult because you can't see where your *feet* are landing. Regardless, I became paralyzed by the fear of hurting myself, particularly my head—not a good thing for a budding gymnast, but I refused to quit. Why? I saw my dad playing tennis with a ferocity that was unstoppable, despite the fact that he had an electrolyte imbalance, and during the hot New Hampshire summers he more than once had to be rushed to the emergency room straight from the tennis courts. His body would be sweating profusely, sometimes to the point where he would pass out. He often tried to cure himself by lying in a tub of cold water. But on a few occasions, we had to drag his naked body down the stairway from the bathtub, and I had to help haul him into the car for a trip to the hospital and intravenous electrolytes.

He refused to let such minor setbacks lessen his drive to win. Like my mom at spoons, he was relentless. And so I came to understand at an early age how such traits carry over to one's strategy at the card table. Starting with my parents and my brother, I learned to read players as a way of forecasting how they would behave in various situations over time. I grew up understanding how people reacted when they had a good hand or a bad hand. I also understood how emotionally unhinged people would get in losing. It happened with me; I threw my cards at the wall every time I lost.

There was something my parents considered even more crucial than cards and competition: education. They would let nothing stand in the way of our learning. And they devoted most of our non-card-playing family time to improving our knowledge.

We used to have something called "Lie With," where my father would lie down with us and read, stopping to teach us what certain words meant and where they came from. So one night, when I was eight, and we were reading *James and the Giant Peach*, we came upon the word "pandemonium." My dad asked me if I knew what the word meant. When I said "no," he patiently explained its root and origins, how the word came from Greek, with *pan* meaning "all," and *daimon* meaning "the abode of all demons."

I remember the exact moment in my life when I learned that word. It was a word that, more than any other, would come to describe my family's little corner of the universe as Mom found less and less in life at St. Paul's that could make her happy, and as I started getting old enough to join my parents and Howard in the pastime that, with more regularity, seemed to take over every spare moment in the Lederer household: playing cards.

5

Sunday, May 9, 2004
4:00 P.M.

BACK FROM OUR TEN-MINUTE BREAK, back from chatting in the alley or consoling one another on the bench or grabbing a quick bite in the buffet, we assemble at our respective tables.

The massive video monitor tells us it's Level Five. The blinds are $100-$200 and the betting limits are $200-$400.

For a few brief minutes, I feel a surge of optimism from my win against Toto. Of course that feeling evaporates when Todd Brunson, mullet ponytail and all, arrives at our table. Then, a few minutes later, Chris Ferguson strides over in his Stetson and boots. These are great, challenging players. Nobody wants great, challenging players at her table. Especially not me. Not now.

But I'm surviving. I'm playing about a quarter of my hands. Winning small pots. Losing bigger pots. At one point, I notice that Chris has a box of mints.

"Hey, Chris, can I have one?" I ask.

He passes them over to me.

On my right is the doctor who worked for the Centers for Disease Control. As I reach in to take a few mints, the guy goes apoplectic.

"Don't use your fingers to eat those mints!" he shouts. "Eat them directly from the box. You use your fingers to touch these chips and everybody else has touched them, spreading their mucus all over them. Pick up those mints with your fingers and it's like putting everybody's mucus into your mouth."

I turn to Chris and say, "That's okay. I'll eat your mucus anytime."

Everyone chuckles, except Mr. Centers for Disease Control. I glance over at the Ladies event and insert my iPod earpieces into my ears. I check the time: 5:35 p.m.

I have made it for five and a half hours without feeling trapped.

But that's the good news. The bad news: I have only $800 in chips. Par is somewhere around $7,500. And the blinds could eat me alive. At this stage, the blinds are $200-300, which means that I have enough for one more bet.

In poker, as in life, it's dangerous to downplay the role of luck and odds. Over the long run a good player is going to win a certain

Cards that look good to you because you've been card dead aren't right for playing.

Also, don't chase bad hands, hoping for a miracle. Don't continue in pots where the chances of you completing your hand are mathematically slim.

percent of the time. In limit poker, that percentage will most likely be less than 60 percent. That's enough to make you all the money in poker that there is to be made. That's a huge spread—and a good investment.

But what happens when a professional goes through a month and wins thirty times in a row? Obviously, that is way out at the tail end of the distribution. It's a statistical anomaly. And it's going to balance out, so that you're going to have a month when you lose twenty times in a row. It's a regression toward the mean—whatever your mean is. Your mean might be winning, but you're still going to have a bell curve that's distributed around whatever your true expected value is.

When pros get on a winning streak, their tendency is to think, "I'm the greatest player in the world. I can't lose because I'm just so skilled." But they're really only winning because they're lucky. They're taking all their 6-to-5 shots, and they're hitting them. To be sure, they're playing better poker than they would on a losing streak because their confidence level is higher and their table image is better. And that affects their game positively.

Because you're on a winning streak, you might have upped your expected value since you're playing with more confidence. But trust me: it's not shifted more than a few percentage points. I hear people tell me they win 90 percent of the time. I say that might be true today, but it certainly isn't true over the long run. Statistically, it's impossible. And if you learn nothing else from me, remember that poker results are just a bell curve. So it works the other way, too. You get a run of bad hands, and eventually the cards will come your way. But you have to know how to play them.

This is such an occasion. I have enough left for one bet.

The dealer tosses me A-Q-J-4. Under normal circumstances, it's a reasonable hand with potential for scooping the pot. But with only $800 left it's a godsend, and it's so much better than the average hand you're dealt in Omaha 8-or-Better. With three players in the pot before me, the bet is raised around to me. It's four-way, which means a lot of equity in the pot.

With a hand like this, it makes sense to go all-in with my last $800. What I need is a straight or a set or a best low. I can win the pot, but only if the board comes perfectly for me. Because the pot is so big, I take the risk. I push all my chips—all $800 of them—into the center of the table.

Nirvana fills my head. The band. "Hello, Hello, Hello. How low. . . ."

For a moment, I can feel everyone's eyes boring into me. Some of the players at the table are my friends, like Chris Ferguson. Some are not. But friend or foe, one thing is certain: all of them want me to lose.

We started out with 234 players. The common goal is to watch every one of them stand up and walk out of Benny's Bullpen before you do. It's that simple. If the board that the dealer is about to deliver

Avoid "trap" hands like A-5, where there are many hands that can beat you on the low, including A-2, A-3, and A-4. Remember, A-2 offers nineteen combinations for making the best low.

fails to significantly improve my hand, there will be one fewer player. It will be me standing up and heading down the escalator, back to Howard's house and to my kids, who are probably watching a video.

I remind myself that life isn't so bad. That no matter what happens, I get to go back and enjoy my kids. . . .

The dealer produces the board: K-10-9-8-7.

I let out my breath. I'm saved. These cards give me an ace-high straight: A-K-Q-J-10. There is no low on the board, and I have the nut high. So I scoop the pot. I end up quintupling up with $4,000, which is about average for the table.

I'm totally renewed. During the next twenty minutes, I win a few more pots. I'm average in chips.

And then, the dinner buzzer.

6

MY DAD'S STUDY was physically and spiritually connected to a dormitory called Kittredge. Floor-to-ceiling bookshelves lined the walls of that study.

In the minutes before the monthly advisor dinners, which were held in our dining room, students would often linger there, perusing his books. And when Howard and I wanted to spend time with our dad—which was basically every night—we would venture into the study, where he would be grading papers, preparing for a class he'd be teaching, or studying for a class he was taking at the University of New Hampshire. He would look up from the papers piled in front of him in a distracted "what-can-I-do-for-you?" manner, and we would beg him to play cards.

More often than not he would push aside his papers, put down his retractable red pen, and climb down onto the floor with Howard and me. In this memory, Katy[1] is too small to be

[1]For a more nuanced, beautifully written account of a Lederer childhood, go out and buy *Poker Face*, my sister's memoir.

on the floor with us playing oh hell or hearts or casino. She's in her bed. And where's my mother? She sits on the white, kelly green, and royal blue plaid couch, flush against the octagonal pine coffee table, mindlessly flipping over solitaire cards, sipping from her glass of Vat 69, the cheapest of scotches. Or she is sitting at the kitchen table, doing the same.

If you wanted to talk to my mother, you brought your own deck of cards, suggested a game of casino, and didn't think about the bottle within her easy reach. Sometimes she played. Sometimes she'd just stare right through you. My mom wasn't always like this—it was the summer before third grade, when my mother got hepatitis. Before that, she had been an attentive mom, helping out at the nursery school, swimming and playing tennis with us at the club, keeping the house immaculate. Dinner would always arrive, hot on the table, when my father got home. She arranged incredible Christmases rife with twelve-foot evergreens and stockings so full with gifts they spilled out onto the floor.

But she had always wanted a different life. She harbored visions of becoming an actress, of growing beyond her roles in campus theater productions of *The Importance of Being Earnest*, *The Bald Soprano*, and *Arsenic and Old Lace*. That wasn't likely to happen in Concord. So she stayed home and played solitaire. Or completed the *New York Times* crossword puzzle in ink in about fifteen minutes. And drank. Especially after she contracted hepatitis, my mom drank all the time.

In the world beyond my dad's study, in the universe outside the Lederer household, the cheerful and confident, buttoned-down and tidy progeny of money yukked it up as they trotted across campus with their lacrosse sticks. Within our four walls, amid the clutter, semi-perpetual war raged on, as unkempt children and their parents dreamed of better times.

Unless we were playing cards.

A card game on the kitchen table or on the floor of my dad's study became the safety zone in my family. It was a separate universe, where we were momentarily happy. Yes, it was pretty much the only time we did anything together as a family. And, no, it was not always peaceful. As the youngest in those games (since Katy was too young to join in), I was more often than not the loser, and nobody really taught me that critical life lesson of how to be a gracious loser. (And, years later, when such a thing mattered, I realized that nobody had actually taught me how to be a gracious winner, either.) So when the score from an oh hell game was tallied and I wound up on the short end, as I usually did, I was the one tossing the cards into the wall or at my brother, tantrum-style, and storming out of the room. Because I always lost, I've spent my whole life wanting—perhaps more than anything else—to win.

But the truth is, for better or worse, my father didn't believe in letting his kids win. His mantra was that we had to earn our win, and he was firmly convinced that this was the best path to creating stronger, smarter, more confident players. Years later, I heard someone ask him if he had ever considered how such an approach impacted his children's self-esteem.

"What's *that*?" he deadpanned.

So from a very young age, I was playing relatively sophisticated card games such as hearts, gin, oh hell, and bridge. Clearly, our household wasn't about go fish. We rarely played poker itself. Maybe twice a year my dad would pull out his plastic chip set and play "pass the trash," a.k.a. anaconda, a poker variant that involves passing cards to other players. (It's clearly not a game ever to be played in a casino, as it would ease the cheating process.) It might seem surprising that two professional poker players grew up in a house where poker was rarely played, but my parents weren't gamblers. We managed to learn everything we needed from those other games.

And while my dad never let us win, he was great at giving us the tools to *learn* how to win. He analyzed every hand the moment it was played. *"Why did you make that lead? You should understand that he had the big club in his hand!"* And we had to have the right answer. When I was thirteen I was asked to sit in on a game of bridge when my dad needed a fourth player. After the evening was over, one of the players turned to my dad and told him that I demonstrated the skills of someone who had been playing bridge for decades.

Come to think of it, our childhood wasn't so different from that of tennis prodigies or violin prodigies.

This was our way of life. In some ways, card playing was the vehicle for teaching us how to think, and in the Lederer household, nothing mattered more. My mom and dad paid scrupulous attention to our schooling, interceding when they felt a teacher wasn't pushing us to learn at the level my parents thought we were capable of handling. Both parents paid a visit to my junior high math teacher when it looked as if a snafu might prevent me from taking algebra at the earliest grade possible. My dad used Howard and me as guinea pigs to test the assignments in English textbooks he was writing. Not surprisingly, I received excellent grades. (When I noted that other kids were rewarded with cash for achieving straight A's, my mom wasn't about to follow suit. "You're a Lederer," she replied. "You're *supposed* to get straight A's.")

If there ever was a breeding ground for two world championship poker players, this was it. We had instilled in us the most vicious desire to win. We continually sharpened our minds. And we learned how people act with cards.

Cards were the glue that held my family together.

7

Sunday, May 9, 2004
6:20 P.M.

WE GET SIXTY MINUTES for dinner; Erik asks if I want to join him for some Thai food (there's a funky Chinese-Thai restaurant called Charlie Vegas a few blocks from Binion's), but I don't feel like Thai. Instead, I go with Boston Red and a few other friends—Artie Cobb, who is still in the tournament but short-stacked, and his wife, Jan—over to the California Club's teriyaki restaurant, a standard-issue eatery of the old-Vegas variety, meaning its carpets desperately need to be replaced. I'm not in terrific chip position, but I'm about par. Just as Artie doesn't have much in the way of chips left, Boston, too, is still in, but barely. By the time we emerge from dinner, the sun has slipped somewhere behind Main Street. The California Club is only about a block away from the ass end of Binion's, but since we've got about twenty minutes left, we stroll around the outside of the hotel to the front entrance.

As we enter the building, the Fremont Street Experience's hourly light show unfolds. Without warning, the underside of the huge arched covering of the Fremont Street mall comes alive with psychedelic colors, followed by a massive set of red lips and an erotically wagging tongue, which appear about four stories above us. "Jumpin' Jack Flash" blasts and explodes into a shower of reds, whites, and blues.

Families stand mesmerized, all eyes focused directly overhead. The Stones are followed by the Beatles, as "Lucy in the Sky With Diamonds" wafts through the evening air and a hypnotic display of yellow and green cellophane flowers floats above us, accompanied by tangerine trees, marmalade skies, and, inevitably, a girl with kaleidoscope eyes. Next comes Hendrix's "Purple Haze," and then a powerful finale of The Who's "See Me, Feel Me." The crowd on Fremont Street applauds wildly.

Down the block to my right is an oversized video monitor beaming a brunette model's vast and naughty cream-smeared smile and the words "Deep-Fried Twinkies $.99." To my left is a kiosk that sells T-shirts announcing, "It's Not a Beer Gut But A Fuel Tank for a Love Machine." If not for the tournament at hand, I wouldn't have any reason to venture into this part of town, which can't seem to escape from under the shadow of the Strip. I think about the arched covering of the Fremont Street Experience. The structure was built to save downtown Las Vegas, but instead it has become a metaphor for the quickness with which digital and visual technology have advanced—taking the rest of Las Vegas with them. That psychedelia-inspired light-show experience feels hopelessly out of date compared to the futuristic spectacles available elsewhere in town.

We step into the excess air-conditioning of Binion's Horseshoe Casino and take the escalator up to Benny's Bullpen.

♦ ♠ ♥ ♣

Soon, a tournament official approaches our table, informing us that we are all moving to different tables to fill the seats of players who have been knocked out. I move over to a table with a lot of people I don't know or recognize. One fellow wears red-framed dark shades, an Ohio State baseball cap, and a large crucifix. He has a nervous way of grabbing his ear. An older man in a maroon polo shirt and enormously thick glasses smacks his thin lips as he peeks at his cards. He twirls an oversized pinkie ring.

The blinds are $200-$400 and the video monitor indicates that there are only twenty-nine players left. We are two players away from the money.

Barry Shulman, the gray-haired publisher of *Card Player* magazine, is at our table. I recently read an interview with Barry in *BusinessWeek* in which he'd said that in order to win at poker, you need to be "selectively aggressive." At this particular table, in the $2,000 Buy-In Omaha Hi-Lo Split event of the 2004 World Series of Poker, I would have to describe Barry's play as "indiscriminately aggressive." Like the Southern gentleman at my earlier table who was briefly winning with hands like 2-2-7-Q (which eventually became his undoing), Barry is playing such hands and *hitting* them.

On the felt in front of Barry sits a huge stack of chips. With $50,000, he is hands down our table's chip leader. Meanwhile, I'm having horrendous luck getting any hand worth playing. I'm card dead, and my stack is holding steady at around $6,000 to $7,000.

From somebody at an adjoining table, I hear, "Oh baby—yeah!" Clearly somebody has narrowly averted being knocked out of the tournament.

Barry is getting in my way. He is literally raising every hand. And even though I'm in late position, I can't steal pots from him 'cause I am undeniably card dead. If I had good cards I could get every one of his chips. He's a roadblock at a point in the tournament when it's easiest to get chips because players are so focused on cashing—in this case, making it to at least the twenty-seventh spot. But mostly I am just trying to stay in the game, watching the more aggressive players battle it out.

I'm not going to play hands that aren't worth playing. Period. You're talking about a game that is all about statistical variation. Sure, any two cards can win in Hold 'em. That's absolutely true. But you don't know when that crap hand—that 7-2 offsuit—is going to hit the board, so all you're doing is taking negative EV (expected value) in order to try to hit a good flop. And if you start thinking that way you're going to start playing too loose, which means playing bad. (Personal note to Dad: I know "playing badly" is grammatically correct, but give me a break. "Playing bad" and "Playing good" are

Don't overplay your hands.

Be selective. In any limit flop game like Texas Hold 'em or Omaha 8-or-Better, you should play only 25 percent of the hands you're dealt. In no-limit games you can increase the number of hands you play because the payoff can be so big.

idiomatic to poker. Remember how much you freaked out the first time you saw me sign an autograph with the words "Play good" as opposed to "Play well"?)

The Southern gentleman, who has been doing so well, gets hit by a reversal of fortune. His aggressive play finally does him in, and he's ousted before the money, before we even get down to the magic twenty-seven players. Who comes to replace him? I look up and see a face I know as well as my own. More or less expressionless. With his relaxed saunter, it is unmistakably Howard approaching our table.

I've been playing poker professionally for a decade now, and I still feel as if I've gotten kicked in the stomach the very moment I re-

Never assume that you should have played a hand.

If you lose a hand, often it's a case where you simply got unlucky. I'll fold 7-2 offsuit all day. So when I do that, and if the board were to come 7-7-2, I'm still not going to bemoan the fact that I didn't play it.

Say you fold two jacks because, based on the way your opponent is playing, you read her as having aces. And then you see the board comes J-3-2. That doesn't make the fold any less correct. It doesn't mean that it was the 1 out of every 5½ times that a jack was going to hit. Do you still want to get your money in getting 2-to-1 pot odds when you're in a 4½-to-1 underdog situation? In a word, no.

alize that Howard and I will be playing against each other in a tournament. This time is no different.

In the past, there was a rule that dictated that relatives couldn't be at the same table until the final table, when there was no choice. For some reason, they changed that rule so that relatives just couldn't start at the same table. The pool of relatives includes Maureen and Bob Feduniak, Milton and Phyllis Meyers, Max and Maria Stern, Doyle and Todd Brunson. There are no other brother-sister pairs that I'm aware of. But there he was, dressed in the same T-shirt and jeans that I'd seen him in that very morning, while we lingered out on his patio with his wife, Suzie, his son, Matthias, and my four kids. It had been a homey Mother's Day scene, complete with hugs and gifts.

Here we are, less than twelve hours later, Howard carrying his $12,000 worth of chips over to my table, where I have $8,000 worth—and we will soon attempt to knock each other out, in pursuit of a prize that exceeds $100,000. Despite his chip advantage, could I ever play soft against my own beloved brother?

No way. And he wouldn't want me to—he'd be offended, and he'd be hurt. Moreover, it would be cheating. If there's one thing my parents taught us it's that you have to earn your win.

Though it wouldn't stop some players I know. There's a lot of money involved in poker, and not unlike the stock market or the corporate sphere, you definitely find people who don't play by the rules. Human nature being what it is, there are some cheaters out there. So, as a professional, you really have to pick your way through and stick with the people who have integrity.

How do people bend the rules at poker? There are people who will play soft with each other in tournaments because they share a financial interest. There are people who downright cheat. They send signals to each other, or they have dealers in the game. Back in the old days of the Dunes in the 1950s and 1960s, cheating was rampant. It was like the Wild West of poker, with players paying off dealers. Cheaters have been part of poker for as long as the game has been around. In fact, in the days of Mississippi steamboats, when it was played with a twenty-card deck and without the benefit of draw cards—you got five cards and had to live with them—poker had the integrity of those games of three-card monte you see on the sidewalks near Times Square. As soon as corporate America took over in the 1970s, the rampant cheating in Vegas card rooms ceased. I feel very safe playing there.

In any tournament, there can be teams of people who essentially play together as a unit. One person might be the backer for five or six others, and whenever he finds himself at the same table as one of the people he is backing, the unwritten rule is for them to play soft against him. Obviously, this isn't always the case, but it does happen—even with some of the best-known players. I won't name names, but most pros know who they are. Here's a clue. A lot of people who cheat at tournaments are terrible live game players because they don't know who to play when people aren't soft-playing them. When they don't have a team and they're just sitting alone at a live game, they tend to suck.

Not surprisingly, a lot of people who don't play honestly are broke. You can think of it as karmic if you want, but you also can see it another way. If you're trying to take edges like that, you likely have the kind of personality that is going to have other problems. Generally, the people who play dishonestly are the ones who have leaks—an addiction to drugs, for example. That's how they wind up broke.

No—I don't soft-play against my brother, despite the fact that he pretty much taught me everything I know about the game. And on each of the three occasions when we've found ourselves at the final table of a tournament, and when I've had the cards to knock him out and have knocked him out, I've always felt badly about it, despite the fact that he handled it with such class. And love.

That doesn't make it any easier to play against him when he joins my table. He has never knocked me out of a final table—but I know there inevitably will be a first time for that.

Will that time be now?

8

HIGH SCHOOL WASN'T A FOND MEMORY for either Howard or me. My brother weighed more than 250 pounds, and the well-bred students at St. Paul's School insisted on calling him "Chowie" instead of "Howie." He had all sorts of social issues, and, like a lot of teenagers of that time, he experimented with drugs and alcohol, and his grades suffered. After graduation, he set out for New York to pursue his goal of becoming a grandmaster in chess. He took a few years' break before starting college in order to immerse himself in chess, but he wasn't able to make a living at it. The same was true of poker. He lived in a card room, sleeping during the day and fetching sandwiches and running errands for the players at night. With the tips he made, he was able to get a stack together to play in low-stakes games, winning enough to keep playing and hone his craft. Eventually, he matriculated at Columbia, but he lasted less than a semester. College just wasn't for him.

While I never made it even halfway to the 250-pound mark,

I was pudgy, too. And not quite the social butterfly I am today. At St. Paul's, most people sort of held me at a distance. And I can't really blame them. Partly it was because they were just so different. Partly it was a matter of my never having learned the social rules. Growing up, my entire universe existed within the four walls of our house on campus. It was a particularly insular environment. None of us in the family—neither parents nor kids—had many friends stopping by. We didn't invite neighboring families over for Sunday dinners and such. The only outsiders who ventured in were students who came for meetings in my dad's den, and basically, they looked at us with something akin to pity, as in oh-you-poor-kids-to-have-to-live-in-such-a-messy-house. Nothing was ever said, but I could sense that we were being looked down upon; you pick up on that vibe. There was another reason for not making the A list (or the B, C, or D lists, either). Our family motto was: Win at All Costs. You don't make many friends that way.

But without trying too hard, I managed to get good grades throughout high school. I was motivated to excel—that's a form of winning, right? I was the student who always knew the answer the teacher wanted, and who managed to get stellar grades without having to cram for tests. I also showed a proficiency for writing. And I was definitely a major thorn in the side of any teacher I felt wasn't intellectually up to the challenge.

At St. Paul's, you had to live in the dorms, and I enjoyed sitting in my room, working out math problems. I loved reading literature—the more experimental, the better. And I absorbed the philosophy texts we were required to read, particularly Paul Tillich, whose book *Dynamics of Faith* helped me adjust my view of the world. He basically says that people who put their whole faith into finite goals like "I'm going to have X amount of money" are setting themselves up for existential disappointment, because ultimately they will reach such a goal and realize their lives still suck.

I tended to socialize mainly with the black students, most of whom were at school under a program called ABC—A Better Chance. They were the only ones on campus who felt more out of place than I did, if that's possible. Setting myself up to be a serious outsider, I spent a lot of time in my room—alone—or in the back stairway near the candy shop, smoking pot.

My family's simmering deconstruction intensified during my high school career, which coincided with the final years of my parents' marriage. My mom was in rehab at one point, and the political waters at St. Paul's had turned chilly on my dad. He and a few other liberal faculty members had flourished under a controversial rector who was something of a business-side guy in that he downplayed religion. When he was replaced by a more religiously focused rector, we suddenly went from required chapel services that were little more than the singing of hymns and the morning announcements to full-scale religious services, four times a week. The new conservative environment became increasingly uncomfortable for my dad. His religion (he was raised Jewish) and his liberalism created a sense of unease. Fortunately, by that time he was writing books on the side (*Anguished English* had started to sell). But he was still at St. Paul's during my high school years.

I enjoyed a few terrific escapes. I spent the summer before my senior year—when I was sixteen—in New York with Renee

Anker, who was just about my only friend at Rundlett Junior High School (where we had been co-outcasts). We both worked temp jobs during the day and partied at night. Then I arranged to spend my winter term in New York, too, working with autistic children at Bellevue Hospital. It was incredible. I felt as though I were really contributing, doing something worthwhile. I sublet a room downtown, near Grand and Essex, in an apartment rented by a friend of my brother's. I would occasionally go to watch Howard play chess or poker, always for money, at various places. He was steadily improving.

Back at St. Paul's, I had earned high enough grades to qualify for magna cum laude. I'd scored well on my SATs. I'd grown up in an academic family. So it was natural for me to take advantage of my strong academic record and apply to one of the eight universities that comprise the Ivy League. But, me being me, I wanted to rebel, and rebelling within the confines of the Ivy League meant only one thing: Columbia. And that meant New York.

I applied for early decision to Columbia. St. Paul's college advisor, a buttoned-down jock, called me into his office after he learned about my choice of university. There, amid Ivy League catalogs, he berated me for a half hour, narrowing his steel-blue eyes and wringing his hands as he implored, "If you go to St. Paul's and you are smart enough, and if you have the grades and the numbers to get into Harvard, *that's where you go.*" Had I thought that he had my best interest in mind, it wouldn't have mattered as much to be chastised over my choice. But the fact was, he was far more concerned about St. Paul's matriculation numbers than about me. They got points for the number of students who were accepted by Harvard.

If I'd had any doubts about wanting to go to Columbia, I was suddenly sure it was the school for me. Plus, my brother was in the neighborhood.

9

Sunday, May 9, 2004
9:40 P.M.

FOUR TABLES LEFT.

Howard is on my left, which is a really bad position for me. He has the advantage of acting after I do. You don't want a good player on your left.

In one of our first hands, I get J-J-2-3. I'm late in the action. I raise. Howard reraises me and I call. The board comes A-5-8, which means I flop the nut low.

The turn is an 8. That pairs the board.

And I check-call.

The river is a jack, which gives me jacks full—with the nut low. This gives me good odds that I have both the high and low. Which means it makes sense to try to trap Howard.

So I check. My brother reraised before the flop, so I know he has a very strong hand. I know he is going to bet.

He bets.

I check-raise him.

He calls. His hand is A-2-4-K. So he had the second nut low, with A-K for the high. And I scoop the pot and really hurt him. This puts me up to around $30,000 in chips, and knocks Howard down to around $10,000.

I can hear someone saying, *"I can't believe she check-raised her own fucking brother."* So I turn around and say: "Are you kidding? I enjoy check-raising him more than anybody else."

The audience laughs.

"Besides," I mutter, "it's the right play."

I love my brother, but not enough to give him my money.

Howard restores himself, winning a lot of chips from Barry. Then Todd Brunson arrives at the table, and both he and Howard start brutalizing Barry. To counter Barry's hyperaggressive play, Howard uses his cold mathematical analysis of hands and Todd relies on his brutal instincts to do the same. Barry began this tournament level as chip leader but, with his freewheeling play, manages to lose it all within a few hours. (Barry ends up getting knocked out twenty-ninth—two people before the money.)

Howard gets drawn to another table.

"Maniacs" are folks who play a super-aggressive, loose style of poker.

Isolate them if you think you have the best hand and then only raise on the river. You don't want to discourage them from bluffing off their money.

I win enough pots when I can to keep my stack at around $30,000, only to get it knocked down. I reach for the iPod in frustration and soon Nirvana's "Lithium" fills my head; "I like it—I'm not gonna crack. I miss you—I'm not gonna crack."

But that doesn't last: I can hear Matt Savage's voice over Kurt Cobain's. I remove the earpiece and hear the announcement: we're now down to twenty-seven players—and all in the money.

I slip the iPod back into my pocket. They don't let you wear headphones when you're in the money. The stakes are too damn high.

There's a round of applause acknowledging the fact that we will all walk away with *something*, ranging from $2,580 for the twenty-seventh player remaining (a $580 net profit over the $2,000 buy-in, barely enough to cover tips to the parking-garage valets and the women who deliver soft drinks) to $137,860 for the last player standing.

A couple of hours and maybe three Diet Cokes later I look up and realize that it's nearly midnight. Mother's Day is almost officially over, my kids long asleep. I recall our morning, which seems so long ago now: Maud, who looks exactly as I did at her age, all dark hair and bright eyes, proudly presenting me with a stickered page of butterflies, mermaids, a palm tree, and the magenta crayoned words "The World's Best Mom." The perfume Leo gave me, encased in neon blue wrapping, obviously bought by his nanny or his dad. Lucy, who, at three, rolled over and murmured, "Happy Mother's Day," then: "I love you." That was gift enough. Then finally Nelly, two, who repeats everything she hears, mumbled: "I love you."

I smile at the memory and look up in time to hear Matt make the announcement that we're down to nineteen players and need to balance the number of people at each table. Once again, Howard moves to mine. But this time, *I'm* on the left. Howard is in the two seat. I'm in the three seat. Not only do I have a position on Howard, but I also have a chip advantage—about $35,000 versus his $16,000. Erik Seidel is also at this table, in the nine seat.

Don McNamara, a forty-year-old businessman in Nikes and jeans, is from Silicon Valley and in the four seat. He enters a pot with my brother. The flop produces a king high. Howard reraises Don to the river to try to isolate him. Then Don checks. Howard checks. Don flips over a pair of kings for the set. Howard looks surprised. "You had kings?" he says. Then he gives me a peek at his hand. Howard had an A-Q-8-8.

"Yuck," I say.

The problem with Howard's hand is that it just isn't very good. It's a hand to pass with, even if you're going against a player who plays too many hands and is inexperienced, which Don clearly is. If you want to isolate a player you need to have a hand that's going to win one side of the pot, and 8s aren't going to do it.

The time to isolate is when you have a hand that's very strong on the low side but has a pretty good way to win the high.

What you're doing is increasing the probability that you'll scoop the pot. But if you counterfeit your low, your high is more likely to stand up against one opponent rather than several. The fewer opponents you're against, the more likely it is that your high side will win.

Howard isn't the only one having a rough night. Someone at our table mentions that Phil Hellmuth was knocked out in twenty-first place by Shadow Hoffmaster, the former PGA golf pro who started playing poker in the late 1990s after a thirty-year hiatus. Apparently, Phil had played a previous hand against Shadow in which the former golfer went passive and folded on the turn. A few hands later, reasoning that Phil had him pegged as a passive player, Shadow used that image to his advantage. Both were short-stacked. Shadow had the nuts, but slow-played Phil, who put Shadow all-in. When Shadow surprised Phil by turning over the better hand, he ended the tournament for Phil. In a reaction that runs counter to his poker-brat image, Phil tapped the table lightly and said, "Nice hand, Shadow."

ESPN takes a break from the action at the Ladies' event to focus their cameras on our table, where brother and sister are poised for battle.

Howard opens the pot with a raise.

I look down to see A-A-10-9, double suited. It's not a great hand—it doesn't offer a guaranteed high and has little chance for a low—but it's a good hand with which to isolate somebody. My thinking is, because I have aces, I have the chance to knock him out of the tournament if I go heads-up with him. And there's a lot of equity in knocking somebody out. So I reraise, to the point of eliminating players other than Howard.

Howard has only about $6,000 in chips. Looking especially professorial, he strokes his chin as he places his last chips in the pot.

Everybody folds.

Howard turns over a pair of kings—no match for my aces.

In the heat of the action, it's the only move to make. But after the hand, the reality sinks in, and it sucks. I knocked my brother out of a tournament, again. The person I wanted to win almost as much as me. This was the third time I had done that in a World Series.

Matt Savage takes advantage of this moment to announce that the World Series will no longer let family members play together again, outside of final tables. For us, it's a little too late. First, I cripple my brother, then I eliminate him. Sure, that means one less player in the tournament. But I feel like a crud.

From behind me, I hear the loud words, *"She's smokin', man!"* I turn around to see a guy with a crew cut and an enormous gut in a purple football shirt giving me the thumbs-up sign.

"Annie, you rule!" he yells.

Howard goes out in nineteenth place. I say, "I'm sorry, Bub," and I really mean it. He takes it well, shrugging it off and wishing me well. And then he strolls toward the exit, to be greeted by well-wishers, whose hands he shakes, both friends' and strangers' alike.

Moments later, he's out of Benny's Bullpen and back on the freeway, heading west.

In Hold 'em, aces are likely to hold up against several opponents, but in Omaha, that's not true. So if you isolate down to one opponent, you've increased the chances that you're going to win.

10

AREA. LIMELIGHT. Danceteria. Save the Robot. The Tunnel. Anyone who passed through New York in the 1980s knows these names. They were the clubs of the decade. And I was there—practically every night. In high school I had been a real loner. A total outie. New York held the promise that I could meet a broader mix of people than those who'd populated my limited universe on the St. Paul's campus. I'm convinced that people who choose to go to college in New York tend to be more eclectic than other students. You probably get a larger concentration of high school outies. And just as New York offered more opportunities to have fun than any other college location I could have chosen, it also offered something highly desirable: anonymity.

At first, I was disappointed by the folks I met at Columbia. While it felt great being away from home and St. Paul's, I had been assigned to Carmen Hall, a freshman dorm, and put on a floor with jocks, who are actually hard to come by at Columbia.

I think the entire swimming team was there. (I felt overwhelmed by the smell of chlorine-soaked Speedos.) I didn't have a lot in common with the swimmers, so I rented an off-campus apartment the first chance I got. It was located at La-Salle and Broadway, just a block south of 125th Street. Harlem wasn't yet gentrified. The apartment got robbed three times, and heroin dealers populated the block. But the rent was right: $615 a month for a two-bedroom. It was dark, but I kept it tidy and I had a succession of roommates, including three cats: Amelia, Franklin, and Twinkie, who was named after a Siamese cat I had growing up.

Amazingly, it wasn't hard to make friends. I was pretty and thin. I was funny and smart. I was nice to people. And before it became a verb, I learned how to party. You didn't need much more than that to become popular.

The fact is, outside the Lederer household, I was learning the social rules. Unlike high school, where I felt compelled to win at all costs—which usually meant getting the best grades—here I was able to focus more attention on meeting interesting people. And everybody was far more interesting than the folks at St. Paul's. The campus was full of kids who were (like me) down to earth, kids who (like me) came from screwed-up families, kids who (like me) weren't afraid to be individuals. In fact, individuality was highly valued.

Starting in 1983, when I was a freshman at Columbia, pretty much the entire focus of my being was to cram as much fun as possible into the hours between midnight and four a.m. most nights of the week. Actually, this was true for a lot of people. Not unlike today, Wall Street was raging with cocaine-snorting twentysomething millionaires. There was always a party, always a crowd for sharing a taxi downtown or a limo back uptown. As long as you looked like somebody, and as long as you dressed the part (which I did—Madonna was calling the fashion shots, and I obliged), you could pretty much get in wherever you wanted.

And much to my delight, folks who had snubbed me at St. Paul's had heard through the post–prep school grapevine that I could get my friends into any club, any time, because I was able to get in myself. Suddenly, these people were calling me up, dying to get together. Classes? I had declared a double major in English literature and psychology and found I could get great grades just by reading the texts or assigned books the week before the exams.

But that was only half the story.

A major reason I didn't go to class regularly was that I started to have a lot of trouble just being in a situation where I was obligated to be there, and to stay, where I couldn't just get up and leave. Restaurants became tough because I had to wait for the check. Movies meant waiting for the credits, though I soon learned that if I sat on the aisle, I could run out, if need be. Class was a different story.

So here's what would happen. I'd go to class and, at some point, once the professor was deep into his lecture, a wave of panic would engulf me. I felt trapped. Frightened. Overwhelmed. I felt an urgent need to escape.

And so, I would. I would run from the room and try to exorcise the feelings the only way I could imagine: I would make myself throw up.

Feelings of anxiety and panic had been a subtext in my life for as long as I could remember, but there was always something external causing them. From the time I was eight, my mother was drinking. I lived in an every-man-for-himself household that was often chaotic, and attended a school where I had few friends and existed primarily as an outsider.

But in New York, pretty much everything in my life was right. I attended a great school, and I was making good grades without investing too much time or effort. I had a lot of friends; I finally felt like I fit in. But the more popular I became, the more anxious and panicked I became. When I wasn't dancing to club music, I was freaking out.

It all came to a head the night of July 13, 1985. I was nineteen years old. I was at my friend Renee's house. She, too, had moved to New York, and later matriculated at Columbia. I just collapsed in tears with her in the bathroom. A bunch of us were watching Live Aid, that historic global benefit rock concert; somewhere between Tom Petty and the Heartbreakers' performance of "American Girl" and Eric Clapton's "Layla," I had a horrible panic attack and ran to the bathroom.

Poised over the toilet, I heard the applause that followed when Phil Collins introduced Led Zeppelin's Jimmy Page and Robert Plant and John Paul Jones. In the bathroom, I felt a wave of anxiety that would not subside. My heart pounded and sweat poured out of my body. I was frozen, terrified, and I didn't want to go on.

Then I heard Renee at the door.

"I'm going to kill myself," I told her. *"I can't do this anymore."*

By that time, my mom had stopped drinking, but her fear and disappointment and how she dealt with them had taught me a valuable lesson. I wasn't going to start drinking or abusing drugs in order to get through the day. I couldn't live that way. I was determined to tackle it much differently.

Everyone in my family had always assumed that I would succeed—and yet, there I was, failing them. I was very afraid to tell my parents that I wanted to go into a hospital. But I knew I had no choice.

As fate would have it, my mom had moved into an apartment across the street from Renee. (After two decades, she had finally left my father to pursue her long-delayed dream of becoming an actress.) She was making the rounds of auditions and selling classified ads at the *Village Voice.* As I climbed the steps to her apartment, I rehearsed the calm and measured way I was going to relay the news. But when she opened the door, I couldn't hold back. I burst into tears and told her everything. She felt horrible, but also admitted that she wished she'd gotten help herself when she was younger.

Next, I called my dad. I was afraid he would be angry at me, so the first words out of my mouth were: "Please don't yell at me about how much this is going to cost." It turned out that my dad didn't care about the cost. He was just worried that his daughter was in so much pain.

The next day Renee and I went to the emergency room at St. Luke's–Roosevelt Hospital. It was drizzling outside, and I remember fixating on the noise made by windshield wipers on the taxis that worked Ninth Avenue. With my best friend there for support, I announced to the admitting nurse that I wanted to check myself in. After some brief discussion, they gave me some Xanax and told me to return the next day, when a certain psychiatrist would be there. Outside, the rain had stopped. The heat, the moisture in the air, and the sedatives made me feel sluggish and confused.

The following day, I returned. I was in that hospital for two weeks, surrounded by schizophrenics, the chronically depressed, people much sicker than I was. Their presence served as a cautionary tale of illness left untreated, and I was glad that I'd reached out for help.

I was diagnosed with a panic disorder and put on Nardil, one of the earliest antidepressants, and given a prescription for Xanax for anxiety. I started seeing a therapist on a weekly basis. Bolstered by medication and therapy, I started to get better. Although the feeling of being trapped in certain situations would become a theme in my life, I managed to have a successful college career.

While I was on medication in college, I couldn't shake the feeling that, because I needed something to help me, I was somehow failing. I wasn't getting better on my own merits. So I got off the medication as soon as I could. And it was hard, but I did it, knowing that if I ever veered off course again, I could do something about it.

It was a lesson that would become invaluable at the poker table, where one's bankroll can depend on the ability to recognize the signs of tilting. Getting emotionally wrought with your losses and desperate to win them back? There's one surefire strategy for ending the madness: call it a night.

Looking back, possibly the most amazing thing about that entire experience was the fact that hardly anybody was aware of my suffering. From the time I was very little, nobody ever knew when I was unhappy. To those around me, I was a party girl with good grades, lots of friends, and New Wave/Punk clothes. By college, I had become extremely proficient at hiding my feelings. I couldn't have known it at the time, but I was training myself for a profession I never dreamed I would pursue. Maintaining a stone-faced exterior is a vital skill for any poker player, and I would say I had turned into an expert. For better or worse, I had been honing that skill every day for most of my life.

I had no real plan for life after Columbia. As a psychology student, my work-study assignment involved providing research assistance to a Columbia professor who had received her Ph.D. at the University of Pennsylvania in the area of psycholinguistics, which involves the study of language acquisition. She had worked under a woman named Lila Gleitman. I met her and she was a wonderful person—very intelligent and confident. Supportive, too.

So, in the absence of a better idea, I figured I'd apply to Penn to study under Lila. My advisor at Columbia offered to write me a recommendation. I took the GREs and did very well. I figured I would become a professor. I figured it was what you were supposed to do, if you're good at school and you have no idea what to do with your life.

So off I went, to study something for which I had no real passion: how children learn their first language. I was about to devote my life to this area—first as a student, then as a professor.

My parents would be proud. I would earn people's respect. I would be happy.

End of story.

11

Monday, May 10, 2004
12:28 A.M.

WITH EIGHTEEN PLAYERS LEFT, we draw to two tables. The blinds are $1,000-$1,500.

By this time, I've built up a comfortable chip stack of about $31,000. I guess the words "guardedly optimistic" would describe my view of the tournament right now.

My dinner companion Artie Cobb gets knocked out fourteenth. He had gotten pretty close to the felt by the time we left for dinner and wasn't able to improve after we returned. Then, with thirteen players left, Don McNamara, the tall, curly haired player with an MBA, arrives at our table. I win a good pot against him and assume I can win more against him, too. (His nervous gestures indicate that he isn't experienced at playing tournaments at this level.)

I get a hand: A-Q-7-2 (all but the queen are clubs).

Everybody folds, except for Don.

He raises before the flop.

I reraise him.

"Jee-sus-Chriiist!" I hear someone yell from the other table. It's what Gus Hansen calls "the hour of the outburst." The combination of long hours—we've been at this for twelve hours—and stress is making everybody just a little bit crazy. The board comes Q-7-4. I have the ace-high flush draw, with queens and sevens. And the nut low draw. Even if he has aces or deuces, I can hit a flush of clubs to win the whole pot or the low to steal back half of the pot.

I can get the entire pot if a queen or a seven hits. If an ace hits, however, I'll be drawing dead for high. But I still have the low cards to get half the pot.

Master the art of appearing disinterested.

Make it impossible for your opponents to know what you're holding—or to predict what you're likely to do at any point in the game. One of the first things you learn is that you (ideally) never show emotion upon winning or losing a hand. There are some obvious reasons for this. Like the fact that emotionally acknowledging your disappointment could dull your play for the subsequent hand. It also could give competitors a slight edge, as in, "She's tilted from the last hand. She'll play this next one like a maniac. I'll take advantage of that by leading into her in the next pot." Alternatively, by openly showing excitement upon winning a big hand, you could propel yourself into a state of overconfidence.

There are only four cards that can beat me. An ace will give him three aces, and I know there's only one ace left in the deck. A 4 will counterfeit my two pair, giving him aces and fours, and there are three of those left. That makes four cards.

So Don is a 9-to-1 dog to get an ace or one of the 4s on the next card. Even if he *does* get one of those cards, I can redraw for the low on the river.

So basically, on the flop I'm a huge favorite—with the high locked up and a huge low draw. I have *twelve* ways to get half the pot back, even if he manages to hit one of the four outs to beat me—I can win with any of the four 3s, four 5s, four 6s, and four 8s. He checks.

I bet. There's $8,000 in the pot.

He calls.

He hits an ace on the turn.

Damn.

Now I'm bargaining with myself, thinking, Okay, if I hit a low card that doesn't give me a pair, I can still win the low. And if I hit a flush card, I can still win the high.

A blank hit on the river. We turn over our cards. His hand is A-A-K-10, which gives him three aces. Against the odds, I lose the whole pot to him; it's a huge blow. I'm bummed, feeling like I might not even make it to the final table.

He removes his wire-frame glasses and rubs his eyes. I think he's a little surprised by his luck. There were only four cards in the entire deck that could have let him beat me, and he hit one of them.

I could tell he was relatively new to tournament poker by the way he was acting, not as confident as a more seasoned player. But he came up to me afterward and said, "I just want to let you know how well you played that hand." In contrast to the way many pros would respond to such a win, he was a true gentleman.

Niceties aside, I'm down to $13,000. And I'm hit with an overwhelming sense of déjà vu. This is not the first time I've lost to one of the very few cards in a deck that could beat me. In 1999, I went head-to-head with Eli Balas, the former diamond merchant from Israel who's won three WSOP bracelets, at the final table of the $5,000 Limit Hold 'em event. We were extremely close in chips, but I was ahead. I held kings and jacks.

The board was K-J-9-8. He had 7-6.

So he made a play on the turn, check-raising me, just trying to pick up the pot.

I called. He was a 6-to-1 dog. There were only eight cards in the deck that could beat me.

The river was a 5, which gave him a straight. Because of that hand I took second place. I would have won that tournament, but I got beat by a single card.

Reraise on the turn.

Why? One, you get a chance to win the pot right there. Two, if you're semi-bluffing and you hit your hand, you win an extra bet. Three, it helps for future hands; your opponents don't know if you're raising on the draw or because you have a good hand. You're much more likely to get paid off with a good hand because they think you're bluffing or semi-bluffing.

Losing that hand to Don McNamara puts me into a semi-panic. I can't stop thinking about the loss to Eli Balas five years before, and the possibility that it might repeat itself if I make it to the final table and go heads-up. For maybe fifteen seconds, I wallow in an attack of the "Oh-God-Why-Me?" variety. I want to race for the door.

My $13,000 in chips is really below par.

Just then, I knock out someone I don't recognize. Then I manage to win a random hand against another guy I don't know, and somehow work my way back up to $44,000. I am exactly on par.

It's 12:57 a.m., and we're now down to ten players. We combine to one table. Kevin Song, a circuit player from Hacienda Heights, California, pushes in all of his chips, and Erik Seidel knocks him out. He's wearing a faded red polo shirt, a black windbreaker and cap, and an expression that broadcasts resignation. Down to nine players means I've made it to the final table.

There's no resting on your laurels in poker at all, and certainly not at an event as competitive as the World Series. I know the toughest work is surely to follow. But for a moment, I'm proud of the fact that I outlasted 225 players. And then, as Kevin Song walks out the door, those who remain stand up to stretch and congratulate one another on our advancement to the final table. In alphabetical order, we're Todd Bleak, Ray Bonavida, Todd Brunson, me, Ron Graham, Shadow Hoffmaster, Don McNamara, Erik Seidel, and Dr. Max Stern.

At a little past one a.m., we're done for the day. All the railbirds and other nonplayers are ushered out of the room as the doors are locked and tournament officials tally our chips, sealing them in plastic bags for tomorrow and requesting our signatures on documents attesting to our chip counts. I officially have $44,000 in chips, which puts me in sixth place. Erik, whose $66,000 puts him third in chips, walks over to me, and I say: "Let's go out for a drink."

Within minutes we're in Sammy's Woodfire Grill. I speed-dial Howard to tell him I'm sixth in chips, which is in the middle of the pack. I tell him how jazzed I feel to be at the final table when I blew off the Ladies tournament. He, too, sounds excited. I order artichoke dip and a Belvedere and tonic. Erik has a beer. We talk about how great it would be to be heads-up at the final table, although we also joke about how we will probably donk off our money before then. Nearby, two Elvis impersonators out for an after-work drink sit very close together, talking in hushed tones. At another table, a group of tourists spends an inordinate amount of time photographing and rephotographing one another with their cell phones.

As we get up to leave our booth, a couple approaches Erik and me for a photograph. They are from Maryland by way of Texas and they're effusive and funny, telling us you need a "leather ass" to succeed at poker. "Leather balls, too," adds the woman. So we pose with the woman with the big yellow hair and massive, obviously nonbiodegradable breasts, and her companion, a tall bald man with a thin mustache and purple velvet suit to match his lady's dress. They offer to buy us another round of drinks and we almost accept, but it's two a.m. and it's time to go home.

Heading back to Howard's house I'm exhausted, thrilled, and anxious about facing my brother. Later, I'll joke to an ESPN producer that Howard had locked me out of his house and that I woke up with the water sprinklers the next day. But it's nothing like that. He slaps me a high-five when I walk in the door. His dogs, too, a pair of pugs, get up to greet me. "Final table!" he says. "You deserve this one. I think you just made a mockery of the Ladies event."

I had made it to the final table in another World Series event. I needed this win, as much for the cash as for the self-confidence. There would be Tae Kwan Do lessons and birthday presents to buy, mortgage payments, car insurance payments. There would be orthodontia bills and college tuition. Meanwhile, my kids were deep in slumber at their uncle's house, dreaming of dancing purple dinosaurs and sword-wielding princes and talking Berkshire rabbits who skirt danger as they search for a safe haven, a warren to call home.

12

THE UNIVERSITY OF PENNSYLVANIA CAMPUS in West Philly is something of an architectural collision, where buildings designed in variations of the Collegiate Gothic style coexist somewhat uncomfortably with postmodern edifices. Solomon Hall, home to the Department of Psychology, is a nondescript three-story brick building erected in 1965, tucked into a quiet courtyard of similar structures near the intersection of 36th and Walnut Streets. It seems a world apart from the rest of the university, the towering "Superblock" dorms, the procession of jocks and global grad students and local toughs, the Kinko's outlets and cheap Chinese restaurants and student bars.

On one wall of the Psychology Department lobby are wood-framed photographs of the twenty-four members of the department faculty, including Dr. Lila Gleitman, with her short-cropped gray hair, exuding brilliance and warmth. To the immediate left is a photo of Lila's husband, Dr. Henry Gleitman, looking patient, insightful, charming, demanding. They are the extraordinary mentors I came to study under while I was here, brilliant people who took me into their hearts and generously shared their time, expertise, and guidance.

It still amazes me to think that, at one point, I, too, could have been among the faces on that wall. But, as the old cliché goes, life is what happens when you're busy making other plans.

I came to Penn to study how the human brain acquires language. I had cultivated the deep mathematical skills required of a psychology researcher, and the ability to plow through hundreds of pages of text in a single night and retain relevant details with almost photographic precision. I also possessed the killer instinct needed to survive in a small graduate program—there were only about thirty grad students in the psycholinguistics group.

Let me correct myself. Looking back, I realize I had too *much* of the killer instinct. Be it in academics or card playing, I had been spoon-fed competitiveness for seventeen years in the Lederer household. That drive to succeed at all costs didn't really surface much at Columbia—as an undergraduate, the field of competitors was large and there really wasn't a single pot of gold over which to do battle. (Besides, I was a bit too caught up in the club scene and my impending anxiety to notice what my peers were up to.) In the Penn psycholinguistics group, however, we thirty were pitted against one another for such rewards as fellowship income. I applied for a National Science Foundation fellowship, which is really hard to come by, and was one of only two students in our program to get one. We got $13,000 a year with which to support ourselves while we studied.

Often, students of a graduate program coexist as a family—studying together, partying together, and celebrating the likes of Thanksgiving together, especially if you're far from home. But within weeks of arriving at Penn, my fierce competitiveness wasn't winning me any friends. Colleagues did their best to avoid me. On the surface, I couldn't see why: I was pretty, (healthfully) thin, and still knew how to have a good time. But nobody wanted me around. In poker, you can play brutally against someone—you *have* to play brutally if you want to win—and then go out with your opponent for a marathon session of blackjack and craps, with multiple Belvedere and tonics, joking about failed bluffs or bad beats. Grad school didn't work that way. Nobody saw my doggedness as an endearing trait. I became very depressed.

Like an unwelcome relative, my panic attacks returned. In a city with more hospitals than shoe stores, I was able to get the medication I needed pretty easily to keep on an even keel. I also started seeing a behavioral-cognitive therapist, with impressive results. The University of Pennsylvania was something of a ground zero for that particular brand of therapy at the time, and I reaped the rewards. The one-two punch of pills and therapy took the edge off my anxiety, and as a result, my competitiveness. It also kept my depression at bay. As I found my equilibrium, colleagues who had shunned me now wanted to study together or catch a movie or go out for dinner. Soon, I was hosting parties at my awesome apartment—four high-ceilinged rooms on the fourth floor of a brick building at the corner of 45th and Pine. I was even playing tennis a few times a week. Each morning I would get up and enjoy the mile walk to the lab. Life was actually pretty good.

But while my life was on an even keel, the truth was I had no interest in learning how children learn their first language. Yes, I enjoyed teaching and got some pleasure out of sitting down to help students during office hours. But there was something missing. Academia was a lover who just couldn't do it for me. . . .

I felt like a fraud. A lot of my peers really cared about what they were studying, and worked so much harder than I did. And here I was, doing a great job but not really caring, not that engaged.

So for five years I taught. I collected and analyzed data. I wrote scholarly treatises about my research in the subject of syntactic bootstrapping, and was within grasp of writing up my research as a dissertation to be titled "Human Simulations of Vocabulary Learning," defending that dissertation before a faculty committee, and then lining up in a West Philadelphia auditorium to be handed a diploma bearing the words that probably still give my father goose bumps: Anne Lederer, Ph.D.

To get jobs in academia, you first have to line up job talks (like the one at NYU that I had to cancel because I couldn't stop throwing up; but I'll get there in a second). I approached the top universities in the field of psycholinguistics, sending off my curriculum vitae—eight long pages that chronicled numerous presentations at conferences and publications in academic journals and other scholarly achievements that my heart was only half in. A half dozen of those universities responded with invitations. In a year when nobody else got any job talks, I got *all* the job talks. Somehow, it didn't matter. I was doing it all because I was good at it, as opposed to liking it.

But, as was the case at Columbia, my academic disinterest could be pushed aside because my social life had become so satisfying. There were lots of friends. One of these was Ben Duke.

At the time, he was living on the third floor of his ex-girlfriend's house. She was a friend of my ex-boyfriend's. Ben had parked himself in Germantown, after the demise of his one-year marriage. Basically, he was just hanging out. True to my family tradition, we met over a game: Scrabble. And just as my mom had felt instantly taken in by my dad, I was immediately attracted to Ben. He was tall and good-looking, with a boyish face and thick brown hair that was combed back, unparted. I fell in love with his laugh. He was quick-witted, charming, adventurous—and as passionate about opera as he was about football. He was eccentric and seemed to have a very devil-may-care attitude, traits that I found attractive.

I became accustomed to hiding my feelings—he did have a girlfriend at the time, and I was dating someone as well—and we became friends (think Rachel, Joey, Phoebe, et al.). We would hang. Go to movies. Dinner.

At one point, he reunited with his ex-girlfriend. Then he decided to move to Montana to hang out *there*. He had grown up in the West, and his father had a 3,500-acre ranch and a beautiful house out there (think Duke of tobacco and university fame). I remember a few days after he left, he called me from the road and asked me to join him. It was a semi-surprise—and kind of a joke. He had definitely expressed interest in me, but we had never been anything more than friends. I said, No, I'm not coming to live with you in Montana. What? Abandon my life and studies? Not a chance, particularly after working so hard to get well.

All the while, Ben and I kept in touch sporadically. Then, in August 1991, he phoned to tell me he was getting married to a woman with whom he had been having a long-distance relationship.

"Do you love her?" I asked.

"No," he said. "But she really loves me. And besides, the person I really want to marry won't marry me." We had already established our own personal code language; I knew he was referring to me. So about a month later, on my twenty-sixth birthday—September 13, 1991—I took stock of my life, trying to imagine how and where and with whom my future would take shape. This particular birthday would be my last as a student, and it marked a turning point. I knew I was happy with my current situation. I had been living in Philadelphia for five years and liked my friends and my studies. But I also knew my life would soon have to change. I was applying for teaching jobs at a handful of universities, ranging from the University of Oregon to Duke University to New York University. Still, I felt a boulder grow in my gut every time I tried to envision my life as a career academic. More than anything else, it must have been a fear of growing up that led me to pick up the phone and dial a number with a 406 area code. When Ben answered, I said:

"Hey, let's get married."

"Okay," he said.

"Well, you'll have to buy me an engagement ring."

"Fine."

"And you'll have to break up with your girlfriend."

"Fine."

"I suppose we should sleep together before we get married."

"Okay."

I had unconsciously planned my escape. Ben would make his way back East. We would plan for our February wedding, but I would follow through with my job talks. We would spend the late winter and spring in Montana, where I would think about my research, but I would keep my apartment in Philadelphia, with the intention of returning to finish my dissertation in the summer. Or maybe not.

13

Monday, May 10, 2004
8:15 A.M.

THIS MORNING, my kids are bouncing off the walls with excitement. They know I made the final table and that I'll be heading back in a few hours, so in the time we have together everybody wants a piece of me. Maud and Leo appreciate the significance of my success in the tournament, while Lucy and Nelly are just happy to hear that their mom is winning.

We snuggle on the couch, and I pull out *Watership Down* for some family reading. Later, we eat sandwiches on Howard's patio. I referee a fight or two, and then hug everybody good-bye and head back to Binion's for the final table, wearing jeans and a gray T-shirt over a pink long-sleeve.

As I negotiate the freeway into downtown Vegas, I anxiously speed-dial a succession of friends, updating them on my status and accepting their congratulations and good-luck wishes.

I arrive at Binion's. Even the valet knows I'm at the final table.

He takes the keys to my rental car, a white Ford Taurus, and says, "Good luck, Annie." A second later, the wheels screech as he pulls into the garage.

The sunshine is intense, and I blink at the blur of well-wishers greeting me as I step into the dark casino. I walk past the poker tables on the ground floor, where an occasional player looks up to offer support. A young guy in a white T-shirt and yellow-tinted shades calls, "Hey, Annie, gimme a hug," flexing well-defined biceps and smiling widely.

I think, What the hell? It's not every day that people treat you like a rock star. He stands up and I hug him, then make my way to the familiar faces at the final table:

Todd Bleak—the dealer-trainer from LA with the handlebar mustache.

Max Stern—the retired doctor who has already won three bracelets.

Shadow Hoffmaster—the retired golf pro who dresses as if he's ready to tee off.

Ray Bonavida—the well-dressed guy with handsome Italian features who's a relative novice.

Erik Seidel—my good friend and backer, and possibly the world's best tournament player.

Todd Brunson—the extra-large player who plays—and wins—some of the highest cash games in the world.

Ron Graham—the quiet-to-a-fault player who can disarm with his shy demeanor.

Don McNamara—the Silicon Valley businessman who has only been playing in tournaments for three years.

The railbirds assume their positions as Matt, in a style reminiscent of TV game shows, announces the names of the players at our final table one by one. He then proclaims that if I come in fourth, I will regain my title as the woman with the most money earned at the World Series of Poker.

It's 2:05 p.m. I glance over to the final table of the Ladies event, where the players—I don't know any of them very well—are surrounded by bleachers and high-wattage lights. Assuming the worst about women, ESPN's cameras are poised and ready to catch a glimpse of the always TV-worthy "catfighting." Most women players I know are too engrossed in the game for that.

The World Series organizers have put us at a nearby table so that ESPN can occasionally swing a camera over to catch our action, or dispatch video photographers with handheld cameras. As we start our final table play, Todd Brunson is our chip leader with $85,000, and I'm in sixth chip position with $44,000.

Eight men and one woman, here's where we stand:

Todd Brunson: $85,000
Max Stern: $79,000
Erik Seidel: $66,000
Ray Bonavida: $55,000
Don McNamara: $51,000
Me: $44,000
Ron Graham: $37,000

Shadow Hoffmaster: $28,000
Todd Bleak: $23,000

Our blinds are $2,000-$3,000 and our betting limits are $3,000-$6,000. At this level, the swings in chips can be fairly dramatic. If you fail to get the right cards, the blinds alone can cripple you—the act of tossing in $3,000 for the big blind can take a major bite out of your stack, and losing a single big bet can spell disaster.

Max Stern is the first to meet such a fate. He and Erik go heads-up in the eighth hand. The board is K-J-5-4-10, with the 10 card on the river giving Erik a straight that wins him a pile of Max's chips. With this single win, Erik totals about $90,000 in chips, taking the lead away from Todd Brunson.

A few hands later, Todd Bleak is on the small blind. He goes all-in.

Ron calls.

Bleak holds A-Q-9-8, with a suited ace.

Ron holds A-K-K-4. Bleak and Ron rise from their seats in expectation. The board comes . . .

A-10-8-Q-J, which gives Ron a straight.

Bleak is out. A good-natured player who lived most of his life in the Las Vegas area before moving to Southern California, he looks a bit like Sam Elliott, the classic American movie cowboy, as he shakes hands with Ron. His win from the Omaha Hi-Lo event of the World Series of Poker: $8,620. A little more than a half hour after we started the final table, we are down to eight players.

♦ ♠ ♥ ♣

Erik and I are in a pot together, and I'm doing what you do in poker: trying to get him to fold. A flush and a straight hit on the turn.

Given the board, which features two hearts, it's likely that Erik thinks I have the best hand. I think Erik has a set and won't call me down, figuring I have a flush. I want to scare him out of the pot, so I raise.

It works. He folds.

"I think you might have just bluffed me," he mumbles.

"No, no, no. I had it," I lie.

This guy is one of my dearest friends, but in poker, I treat everybody equally.

I lie to them all.

Now we get new blinds—$2,000-$4,000—and new limits—$4,000-$8,000. I'm a little above par in chips. I've got a pair of kings. Don McNamara raises and everyone folds to me. I reraise. He calls and I three-bet. We see the flop. It's a 9-10-K. I've got a set of kings, which I think will hold up.

On the turn, Don checks. I bet. He calls. There's no low on the board, but because there are two diamonds, I put him on a flush draw. The river brings a diamond. He checks, looking at me. I check, assuming he has a flush, and turn over my cards. "All I have is a set of kings," I say. He mucks his cards.

I advance to $100,000 in chips.

If you're bluffing, it's better to take the aggressive stance by reraising. If you only reraise with good hands, people will always fold to you.

There's an irony to winning this important hand. A couple of hands later, Don says, "You were so lucky. I mucked the winning hand." Then he explains that he is slightly dyslexic, and that he read the board too slowly to realize that he had made a flush on the river that would have beat my set of kings if he hadn't tossed his cards in the muck. "I had a brain freeze," he admits.

A few hands later, I pick up $22,000 by winning a pot against Shadow Hoffmaster. I tie Ray for the chip lead at about $122,000.

For a moment, I think about what happened at the Bellagio tournament a month before. It was the $2,500 Buy-In Limit Hold 'em event in the Bellagio Five-Star World Poker Classic/WPT Championship. I started out in the middle of the pack and eventually got the chip lead, which I held on to 'til the end. I'd like to be clear: I won that tournament—and $157,000—in large part because I was getting extremely lucky hands.

When poker players are winning, they tend to focus on how great a player they are. When they're losing, they tend to over-

Particularly in Omaha, where there are so many cards to read, even professionals sometimes have trouble reading the board and their hands to see who wins.

When in doubt, turn over your hand. Also note: it's considered the poorest of etiquette to "slow roll," that is, to make your opponent squirm by taking your time turning over your winning hand.

emphasize the role of luck. The fact is, no matter how skilled a player you are, there is still luck in poker. Despite what some pros will tell you, there literally is no player on earth who ever has won a tournament by outplaying everybody. That's not to say winners don't have a lot of moments when they do outplay their opponents, but in the end you have to hit some hands, too.

Because I'm getting decent hands, I start to think that this might be a repeat performance of the Bellagio tournament. But I know I can't count on it. That would be death.

Before I know it, Shadow Hoffmaster is in the small blind and pushes his meager $6,000 chips all-in. Ray and Todd call. The flop comes: 9-7-3. Ray bets and is called by Shadow. Then the turn comes: an 8.

Ray check-raises Shadow. The river is a jack.

Ron scoops the pot with A-2-J-J. He has the nut low and a pair of jacks. Without letting us see the cards that inspired him to go all-in, Shadow gets up to leave. He tells us what his wife told him just before he flew down from Missoula for the World Series of Poker: "She said enjoy yourself and do your best. I did both," he says, slightly tipping the white visor that sits atop his gray hair. He takes home $12,920.

Now we are seven.

A steady tide of spectators washes into Benny's Bullpen and migrates over to our side of the room, hanging behind the velvet cord and occasionally shouting out words of encouragement to friends or loved ones at the table. Reporters, most of whom represent poker Web sites, wander up to our table, jot some notes, then make their way over to the Ladies final table to track the action.

Max and Ray compete over the next hand. Max, who was crippled by Erik maybe an hour earlier, can't hit anything, when suddenly he goes all-in with his hand of Q-Q-9-8. Ray holds A-5-6-8. The board gives him two pair and a six low.

So the doctor, wearing a WSOP jacket, makes his exit, winning $17,220, making us six.

From the moment Max Stern leaves the room, I'm on a roll. The cards are coming and coming. Anything I play seems to meet the flop. I'm on the button, holding 4-6-8-8. It's a highly unattractive Omaha hand because middle cards don't offer much promise for either high or low. Regardless, I play the hand—on the button, I'm in a powerful position.

The flop is A-A-7-7. Ray checks. I bet. He calls.

The turn brings a 2. He checks, I bet, he calls.

The river is an 8. I scoop with a better low and a set.

I'm now solidly in the lead with $150,000 in chips. This is a huge win, and I'm feeling hot.

♦ ♠ ♥ ♣

Ray makes a wheel and I get knocked down to $130,000. Suddenly, we're about even.

Then I lose a few hands where I raise and don't hit the boards. I'm down to $73,000 in chips. I steal a few blinds, and then I'm up to more than $100,000.

A few hands later, I look down at my cards and see A-Q-10-3, with the ace of hearts. The board comes: it includes a K-J of hearts. I'm totally excited—but I maintain my veneer of disinterest. Ron puts me all-in. What I need is an ace, queen, 10, or 9 for a straight. Or any heart for a flush. And because there is a low card in the flop, I can also hit a low.

It's a potentially huge hand and I know I'm a big favorite. That said, I only have ace high at this point, when I opt to go all-in on the turn.

But consider the odds. With two cards to come, there are *twenty-one cards* in the deck that can help me. Thirteen cards is even money, and I have twice that. I feel as if all eyes are on me.

The turn is a low card—that gives me outs. Now there's one card to come—twenty-one cards that will allow me to scoop the pot and twelve cards that will win me half the pot.

I'm the favorite to win this hand.

The river: a nine of spades. This gives me a straight and I scoop the pot, doubling my chips to more than $200,000.

I am back in the lead.

Soon after, Don opens the pot with a raise and Ray three-bets it, putting Don all-in. The board comes 4-4-2-5-3, giving Ray a wheel that beats Don's pocket kings.

Don's out of there. He wins $21,520.

Now we're five.

14

ONCE A FLOURISHING RAILROAD TOWN surrounded by orchards and ranches, Columbus, Montana (population 1,500), is one of those interstate-exit villages that has seen its heyday but still manages to survive. The Slumpstone-faced buildings that line the town's one-sided main thoroughfare might be crumbling with age, but, unlike their counterparts on Main Streets throughout the heartland, they are mostly occupied. There's a drugstore, a hardware store, the taxidermy-abundant New Atlas bar (Ben's home away from shack in his early days in Columbus), the real estate office. The town sags a bit around the edges, but still has a little kick. It's modern enough to boast *both* a chiropractor *and* an acupuncturist, but old-timey enough that you have to drop off your dry cleaning at the hardware store; from there it is shipped to Billings—fifty-one miles east—and returned exactly one week later. (This little inconvenience drove my mom nuts when she and her boyfriend Dale eventually moved to the area to be closer to me, after living in Las Vegas when Howard moved there, and helping with his sports-betting business.) But face it: who really *needs* dry cleaning in Montana?

Columbus functions as a commuter town for the Stillwater Mining operation, some forty-five minutes away in Nye—the only source of such strategic minerals as platinum and malignium in the United States (the only other mine for such minerals is in Russia). There's a metals refining and silversmith operation in Columbus. The town is also a center of outdoor recreation, with the awesome Beartooth Mountains maybe an hour's drive away, and Yellowstone National Park about two hours away.

A river runs through this chapter of my life. Not the Yellowstone, Stillwater, and Rosebud, which converge in Columbus, but the river known as fifth street.

After leaving West Philly, Ben moved to Columbus to be close to his dad, a gentleman rancher with a wonderfully optimistic approach to life. Ben had bought a tiny, no-frills, white house of chicken wire and stucco on the edge of town, just opposite the Burlington Northern tracks and the Yellowstone River. Just a standard four-hundred-square-foot affair that was a bit too close to the double-wide next door. A handful of cottonwoods stood outside. The white paint peeled, the outdoor steps crumbled, the roof leaked. We had to pull a Frankenstein breaker to turn the lights on. There was no shower, and we could fill the tub with only an inch of hot water, which was particularly rough during the long Montana winters. This is where we lived when I joined Ben. Basically, we did nothing. I was hiding from my life and from an uncertain future.

I had kept my apartment in Philadelphia, because I had planned to return to finish my Ph.D. But for the moment, I was hanging out in the county seat of Stillwater County, Montana, and I was sick. All the time. The puking episode that began in my mother's apartment and permanently delayed my NYU job talk never totally subsided.

The doctors in Philadelphia had diagnosed me with something called gastroperitonitis and put me on a cornucopia of medications, things like Reglan and Prilosec, which at the time were not sold over the counter. They prescribed serious doses and I downed them religiously, but still I remained very ill. I had trouble keeping food down, and often experienced severe stomach pain.

This was the condition in which I was married in Grandma Betty's elegant old home in Darien, Connecticut, before we moved to Montana. My wedding, on a bone-numbing February afternoon in 1992, was the first time my entire family had been under the same roof in the nearly eight years since Howard left St. Paul's for New York and a life of chess, poker, and sports betting.

We were happy to see everyone. Happy, too, that Ben was able to wear shoes for the ceremony; a few weeks earlier he had dropped a pot of pasta on his foot and it was touch-and-go until the last day or so. (His mother, unable to face her ex-husband, refused to attend the wedding.) I wore a coral pink Chantilly lace dress (I'm not really one for white, as you might have gathered), and spent the hours before our nuptials in an upstairs bedroom trying not to barf as my mom, Dale, and Katy did their best to calm me down. I was pale and thin, mortified that I might puke at my own wedding. Amazingly, I made it through the ceremony—and the entire day—without incident.

It actually ended up being a pleasant occasion, with a minimum of tension among the family members.

Our honeymoon consisted of driving a Ryder truck bearing many of my belongings cross-country to Montana. The only diversion was when the truck broke down in Deadwood, South Dakota, where gambling is legal. We didn't bother to visit any of the many storefront casinos. We were honeymooners.

In Montana, we didn't *do* anything. I was always sick. Ben was happy to sit around and listen to opera or follow the Denver Broncos in the sports pages. We were scraping by on trust-fund payments of less than $1,000 a month. This all sounds awful looking back from this stage of my life, but back then it was sort of romantic. We had adventure, and we had each other. That, and three channels on our discount-store television.

One afternoon a few months after we had married, we were sitting around, half watching Phil Donahue on daytime television. His guest, Sid M. Wolfe, the author of *Worst Pills, Best Pills*, was talking about his book. We started paying full attention.

Wolfe talked about the worst pill (at least at that time) for causing anxiety. I was familiar with the name because it held a prominent place in my medicine chest. In a flash, it struck me: the doctors in Philadelphia, a city that prides itself on its hospitals and doctors almost as much as on its hoagies and soft pretzels, knew about the anxiety component to my illness, yet they prescribed what I now learned was the worst possible drug for *inducing* anxiety.

Wolfe began rattling off the identities of other drugs. Unfortunately, too many of the names sounded familiar to me. Every single pill I was taking was up there on the chart that was now displayed across our TV screen. There was Ativan. Reglan. Prilosec. These were drugs that were supposed to make me feel better—but they were some of the worst ones I could have been taking. Particularly Reglan, which is related to a psychoactive drug. I heard Wolfe say it can cause anxiety in some people. I was livid.

I made an appointment to see a gastroenterologist in Billings. He told me I needed to get off those medications without delay. He added that if, after discontinuing the medications, I still had problems, he could treat me with erythromycin, which he said had been highly effective for people who suffered from stomach problems. I thought: *All these months, I could have been taking an antibiotic?!*

I'll never forget this time. The doctor's visit was on a Thursday. The following night we were scheduled to drive down to Las Vegas; Howard was still living in New York at the time, but he'd flown out to play in the World Series of Poker. He'd become very good at the game, and he offered to put us up in the Golden Nugget for the monthlong tournament. (It's not as if we had anything else going on at the time.)

I was worried about the two-day drive, worried that giving up my medications might somehow induce a panic attack or severe stomach pains somewhere in the middle of Utah. Luckily, that didn't happen. In a way, Vegas ended up representing something positive, a new start.

Within days, the medications were washing out of my system. I had started feeling somewhat accustomed to my new life, no longer paralyzed by the panic that accompanied this major life change. And it was a thrill to watch my brother compete in the world's biggest and highest-stakes poker tournament in Binion's Horseshoe Casino. On a few occasions, I played a little blackjack.

Howard and I sat down in the Binion's coffee shop between tournaments. It was late afternoon and we hadn't eaten lunch. I had been watching Howard succeed at the table and really loved his passion for the game. As we talked, I realized I wanted some of that passion for myself. So he took out a napkin and wrote down a list of the starting hands—the combination of hole cards that would be good enough for entering a pot. While my brother returned to watch the WSOP, I finished my steak, stuffed the napkin into my pocket, and walked down Fremont Street to the Fremont Casino, which had the lowest-stakes poker around. Binion's had low stakes, but not as low as the Fremont, where I could play $1-$3. Sitting around the table with a bunch of strangers was a bit like sitting on the carpeted floor in my dad's study. It somehow felt right. And there was the camaraderie I remembered from playing cards as a kid.

I played all night and won $300. The best part? When Howard started telling his friends about my winnings. I could tell he was proud, and I was thrilled by that.

With this auspicious start, Howard wanted to encourage me to explore the possibility of taking poker seriously. So he put up the $1,000 buy-in for me to play in the Ladies tournament. It was a lot less than the $10,000 required for the main event, but enough for me to get freaked out about the amount of money at risk, especially since we barely had enough to cover the mortgage.

As the event approached, my anxiety overwhelmed me. Downstairs in the Horseshoe Casino, my stomach started convulsing and my hands trembled. Just as the play was about to begin I raced into the women's room to throw up. As I washed my face and caught a glimpse of myself in the mirror—I looked gaunt, with dark rings around my eyes—they announced that the event was about to begin.

It was everything I could do to get myself to the table. But once we started playing, my panic subsided and I did okay. Not great, but all right for a total beginner.

And that was my first flirtation with poker. Playing was better than sitting on the sidelines, but not sensational. I didn't give it another thought.

I returned to Philadelphia that summer for two hot and muggy months to finish the research for my Ph.D. Then, with its trunk weighed down by cartons of research documents, I drove the Honda back to Montana. I would write my dissertation in Big Sky Country, and then fly back to defend it. That was the plan.

Back home, I shoved those cartons in the shack's sole closet. And I never looked at them again.

♦ ♠ ♥ ♣

In Montana, my health had improved, but our living conditions had become impossible. We didn't have any money. Well, we did have Ben's trust income, which was in the range of \$9,000 to \$10,000 a year. But that's all we lived on. With that as our single source of income, even our monthly \$125 mortgage was hard to pay. We weren't about to starve to death—

Ben's father occupied a splendid ranch about seventeen miles down the road in Absarokee and would have seen to it that we didn't—but as the charm and adventure of our early romance gave way to frustration, it dawned on me that I actually didn't like living like that, with no ambition, no money, and no interest in opening up those cartons to sit down and write the dissertation and become the Ph.D. I always thought I should become. And there was nothing looming on our vast horizon suggesting that our condition might change for the better.

I was frustrated. Bored. Tired of living like that.

One late afternoon, which looked a lot like every other late afternoon, I was particularly antsy. I literally couldn't sit still.

"Shit," I finally said to Ben. "Let's go into Billings to mess around."

Poker was legal—if highly restricted—in Montana card rooms, and Ben's brother George enjoyed playing in some of them.

The thought had occurred to me slowly, but then it was there, bright as day.

"Hey," I said, "let's go play some poker. . . ."

15

Monday, May 10, 2004
4:10 P.M.

WE'RE STILL FIVE PLAYERS.

The blinds are now $3,000-$5,000 and the limits $5,000-$10,000.

From a betting perspective, I have the best seat at the table. Erik and Todd are the most aggressive players, and they're on my right. You want aggressive players on your right because you have the benefit of seeing them act before you. Ron Graham, whose chip stack, like mine, is in the $200,000 range, is playing very tight. He's on my left—exactly where you want a tight player to be, because it makes it easier to sway his action. Todd, who started the final table a chip leader, is short-stacked. Erik knocked him down to $30,000 by flopping a set of jacks. Ron, by the way, is a very good Omaha player, but it seems to me that he may be card dead. He's playing more of a ring-game style, and he's not adjusting well to the short-handed situation. (A ring game is when you're at a full table, and that demands a much different kind of play than a short-handed situation.) Having fewer people at the table requires you to be more active. There are two mathematical reasons for this: one, there are fewer cards out against you, so your hands go up in value; and two, the blinds come around faster when you have fewer players, which forces you to play more hands. You could go broke on the blinds alone, so when you get short-handed, you always have to play faster.

I soon find myself in first betting position, with A-Q-2-4, a very powerful hand. I raise, and Todd calls out of the blind. The board comes J-10-8 (two of them are spades). Todd check-raises me.

It's time to consider this hand from Todd's position. I assume he's thinking that because I raised in early position I'm holding a strong low. That would make sense, because if I'm opening the pot in an early position, I'm likely to be holding cards with very low potential, like A-2. He's not sure what my other two cards are, but he knows that my hand probably has the low. The board comes high. So I feel as if he's bullshitting by raising me. I have an A-Q in my hand, and a back-door low possibility—I have a gut-shot. So I call, thinking there's a good chance he's bluffing, thinking that I can possibly take it away on the turn.

The board pairs tens on the turn. He bets out and I raise him. (I just feel that he hasn't really hit high, that he's just trying to take me off a hand that was clearly going low—because I had raised in early position.) So I raise him and he folds right away.

I read the situation correctly.

I had nothing in my hand.

In Omaha, the best time to bluff is when you think your opponent is going for low. This is what Todd was trying to do against me. But I *re-bluffed* him on the turn and it worked. His playing of the hand would have been great—except for the fact that I put him on that play.

When I made that play against him, I wasn't playing because I thought I had the best hand. I was playing because I felt that given the way Todd had played, it was very likely that he was playing *my* hand, as opposed to his. So I came back at him and played *his* hand.

That doesn't mean Todd played the hand poorly. He didn't. He played it quite well, actually. It's just that I recognized what he had done and then just made the exact same play right back at him. So the same play occurred twice in the hand, once by him and once by me. And I just happened to be the last person to make it.

Regardless, I took a lot of his chips on that hand. And I was up around $260,000.

People sometimes forget that in poker you're actually playing the other person's hand. You should be more concerned with their cards than with yours. This may be common poker advice, but it's also something that most beginning players find difficult to follow, or tend to forget.

Too many people, when they start playing poker, play only their own hands—they get caught up in their own cards and don't spend much time trying to determine what their opponents are holding. So it's always a big leap for a new player to start thinking about what the other person's bet means, and to try to narrow down what that opponent is likely to hold—and to play based on that.

If I think you're not very experienced, I'll play small-pot poker: I don't want to get all my money in before the flop, because I think I'm a better decision-maker than you are. I want to stretch out the play to make as many decisions as I can—that way, I have more opportunities to outthink and outplay you. That lowers the variance and makes it less of a gamble. A novice would probably want the opposite—for me to get my money in early to keep me from making too many good decisions.

Since a lot of how you play a hand has to do with what you think the other people at the table have, it's very important to decide whether you think you have the best hand or you don't. It definitely affects the way you're going to play the hand against your opponent. If you flop what you think is the best hand, you're going to think of ways to maximize the amount of money you can get from the pot. If you think you have the worst hand, you're either going to fold or try to figure out a way to bluff the person, depending on how strong you think *they* are.

So the value of your hand can only be rated in relation to what the other players have. That includes if you have the nuts. If you have the nuts, it's extremely important to know if your opponent is weak or if they're strong. Because if your opponent is weak and you have the nuts, you do what you can to induce them to catch up.

Remember that there's future equity in showing bad hands on a bluff.

You'll get more action on your good hands and make more money. Think of it this way: as a poker player you're a business and you have to have an advertising budget; that's what bluffs are. When they don't work, they advertise the fact that you're unpredictable.

You're going to play the hand very differently than if you think *they think* they're strong—at which point the maximum way to get money out of the hand is to play your hand fast and let them play fast against you. So it's extremely important, no matter what you have, to have a very good read on what your opponent has. Narrow their hand down. Otherwise you'll never maximize your earn.

Hand in hand with that, at any given moment it's really important to be aware of what your opponent's bet is likely to mean. Thinking about betting into somebody? You should clearly decide whether you want them to call or fold. You should look and see if your bet is likely to entice them, and, if so, if they would be "pot-committed" from here on in. If they are pot-committed, they've got too much vested to fold. In those situations, you don't want to bluff. If you do, they're unlikely to fold.

When you're thinking about calling with a marginal holding, you need to look at how many chips you can actually win. The reason: it's critical to get big implied odds. You should be less likely to call with a marginal holding against a short stack because the upside isn't that great.

After losing that pot to me, Todd goes on a roller coaster. He will later complain about a lack of cards, but for the time being, his towers of chips are rising and falling. At one point, he goes all-in and survives. Then, finally, he's in a pot against Ron. The flop comes Q-10-6.

"Great flop," Todd says.

"I could beat it, I know," Ron replies.

He was right. While Todd showed an A-K-K-J for a wraparound straight draw along with his kings, Ron beat him with Q-10-J-7—he had top two. Todd left in fifth position, winning $25,840.

Now we're four.

This is an important moment for me. From the daily printouts of the tournament statistics, I know that the person who ends up in fourth place will win $30,140. Fourth place is the worst I can do. And I have calculated that if I were to win $27,041, I would regain my ranking as the all-time ladies money winner, eclipsing Nani Dollison, who until now held the record as the woman to win the most money at the World Series.

Dollison, a petite former dealer from Hernando, Mississippi, in her early fifties, has won a total $545,550, including first place in the 2001 WSOP $2,000 Limit Texas Hold 'em event, which earned her $441,440. I have been in second place, with a total of $518,509, despite the fact that I've advanced to more World Series final tables than any other female player. Always the tournament bridesmaid, I've made it into the money twenty-two times and had twelve final table finishes.

I did it. I could once again call myself the highest WSOP money winner among women. Of course, I still didn't have a World Series bracelet and I still needed to scale a massive wall and crawl through a jungle in order to get one: I was up against four brilliant poker players, and they wanted nothing more than to win the bracelet for themselves.

And now it's time for Erik to get back at me for my bluff against him. Technically speaking, what happened wasn't a bluff—or even a semi-bluff. It was possible I had the best hand, since I was holding two pair. And in an eerie coincidence, the board is almost identical to the one in my previous hand against Erik: a flush hits the board. Once again, I raise, trying to get him to fold. But this time it doesn't work. I should have known that it wouldn't. Erik has agonized over that previous hand, convinced that I had bluffed him. This time, he calls and turns over his set.

Ouch.

I have a lot of chips ($240,000) at this point, so it doesn't hurt that much. But it *does* hurt.

Erik very carefully stacks up $16,000 of my chips.

I think I might have caught Erik, self-satisfied, grinning slightly. But I just keep thinking that I have to be careful.

Bluffs aren't supposed to work all the time.

It's a percentage play. If you never get called on your bluffs, you're not bluffing enough. If you're getting called every time, you're bluffing too much.

16

IF YOU REALLY PUSH IT, you can make it into Billings in thirty-five minutes. The scenery isn't much to speak of, mostly hills of dried grass in a thousand shades of brown. Montana's most populous city (population 90,000) is lodged between yellow buttes. When you enter from the west at dusk, as Interstate 90 jogs to the right, the thousand shades of brown are replaced with a thousand lights and the promise of something—anything—different. They call Billings the Magic City. No joking.

Soon you're amid the wide, dusty streets of downtown Billings. You park your Honda on the street, and depending on which way the wind blows, you sometimes get overwhelmed by the odor of the local refinery—or is that cow shit? I never could tell. You hear the lonely whistle of a train plowing through the city on the Burlington Northern tracks.

Montana has had poker for as long as it's had white settlers, although as a form of gambling the game has been legal only since 1989. On the wall in a Billings restaurant is an aging photo of a frontier gambler, Canada Bill, posing in front of a bar, with the words "It's morally wrong to allow suckers to keep their money." Below it, Canada Bill's Supplement: "A Smith and Wesson beats four Aces."

The Crystal Lounge is a one-story structure that occupies the prime intersection of 28th and Broadway. You enter the lounge, with its curved bar topped with orange Formica, its red-leather bar stools, its cluttered walls bearing photographs of entertainers from the latter half of the twentieth century (with a heavy emphasis on the 1950s and 1960s). There's Marilyn. Elvis. The Rat Pack, with Frank, Dean, and Sammy puffing on cigarettes. There's even Janis posing joyfully (drunk? high? both?) in front of the Chelsea Hotel. A strip of red light sets a sinful tone. In the rear is a modest dance floor that doubles as a karaoke stage. Sometimes, a one-man band named Ray Dudley croons country songs, accompanied by his own guitar and rhythm box. Tonight, on the video screen, Chaka Khan sings "I'm Every Woman."

Turn right and head downstairs into the finished basement, a smoky, dirty, no-nonsense paneled room with low ceilings and a couple of small (by Vegas standards) green felt poker tables. It feels as if you've stopped over at someone's house and wandered into the room fixed up to serve as a retreat for teenagers. You almost expect to see a Ping-Pong table or a bowl of M&Ms.

This is where I learned my trade.

Later, they would move the poker tables into the "casino" adjacent to the bar and I would play there. It's a paneled room, half of which is taken up with fourteen poker slots and the other half with the poker tables. With its free baskets of popcorn and its microwave oven sitting behind the cash window (to heat up leftovers for the dealers and house players), the place has its own warmth, and playing there was almost like playing in someone's kitchen.

The first night we arrived, Ben hung out by himself, making friends with the locals, which is a particular talent of his, while I moved on to the poker tables. With great deliberation, the tall, balding man in charge counted out the tens and twenties that comprised my fifty-dollar bankroll, and then handed me a plastic tray of chips. Players looked up at me blankly. All of them were men—central-casting retired ranchers and construction workers and cowboys and insurance men, I would soon learn, all settled in for a night of poker and Budweiser. When I sat down among them, their stares took on an odd combination of curiosity and indignation. It was as if a three-toed sloth had just wandered onto their ranch and was about to unsettle the cattle.

On the one hand, it appeared as if they were resentful that I would be penetrating their private little huddle (see, I was already learning to read the other players at the table). But they also seemed to be wondering why a young woman would *want* to sit down and just hand over her money to them. A construction worker still in his hard hat asked the proprietor for "two more Jack and Cokes" (Jack Daniel's, that is) to replace the two that had been drained and were resting, empty, on the felt in front of him. Then he looked at me with half-closed, drunken eyes, and made his best attempt at a wink.

It suddenly hit me: they thought I was there to be seduced!

While the other players were less than welcoming to me in those first few minutes—there was a guffaw having to do with the penis size of one of the players (maybe even mine)—I felt surprisingly comfortable in my own head. We were playing cards, and there was nothing like it for making me feel at home. There I was, matching wits over a fistful of cards. I always loved that feeling. Even with these men-are-men-and-the-sheep-are-scared types.

I kicked off my shoes and tucked my feet under my butt—just as I did in my dad's study—and got settled at the table. It's the best way I know to feel comfortable playing cards. The dealer tossed me an A-Q. I raised. I knew enough about poker to know that with any given hand several of the players would immediately deem their cards unplayable, tossing them face-down into the muck before even seeing the flop. But, perhaps fearing that such a lack of aggression would appear not quite macho, every single player held on to his cards for that first hand.

The flop came A-2-Q.

I bet—possibly a bit too hesitatingly—on my pair of aces and pair of queens. An older player, a guy in his sixties with thinning hair, ruddy skin, and a semi-permanent frown—and a massive gut—slouched in his chair and raised me. Three other players stayed in.

The turn was a 10.

I bet and was raised. One player folded.

The river: a Q. I bet. The others called.

My full house won, and the dealer pushed about $50 worth of chips in my direction.

I had been in the Crystal Lounge for less than ten minutes and had already doubled my money. I loved myself! My panic seemed far away. Okay, so it wasn't a million dollars, but for the moment, my worries about our finances vanished as I stacked my chips in neat little towers.

Then I heard grumbles. I looked up from my chips to catch the guy in the hard hat pantomiming a French kiss. Or was he offering a preview of his notion of oral sex? It was hard to tell. I looked back down at my cards and focused on my game.

It went this way for two hours. Periodically, Ben would amble over to see how I was doing. I won some pots. I lost some pots. It felt good to have him there for the moral support. Then he announced that he would be heading out to check out the bookstore and the record store before they closed. I was on my own with the boys.

I started noticing some patterns in their play. Mostly, it boiled down to this: it was bad enough for these guys to lose their money to *guys.* But they certainly didn't want to lose it to a woman. I must amend that. Over at the other table, an older woman named Kathy—a ranch-mom type—started playing. She seemed to be raking in her share of pots and appeared to be getting along well with all of her male opponents. She was chain-smoking Merits and drinking Budweiser, and I heard her say patiently to one of the players, "No, I think it's fine that you're drunk. It's just profanity that's not okay." It was an impressive display of assertiveness—the kind they used to teach in workshops in the 1970s.

Back at my table, there was no such diplomacy. The more I started winning, the more I seemed to inspire chauvinistic behavior from the men who were losing their money to me. Even before I sat down my opponents had detected that I wasn't a Big Sky State native. My speech lacked the local unhurried cadence—I talk fast, particularly when I'm nervous, and I have a slight uptick—and even if they hadn't heard me open my mouth, they could tell I wasn't homegrown by the stylized cut of my designer jeans. If nothing else, poker players are keenly observant (yes, even these guys), and as they read me for even the slightest of tells, I could see them also reading me for proof that I was different (and not to be trusted): I was an Easterner. I was Ivy League educated. I was, from their perspective, a Jew. Female, too.

I was practically an alien.

They didn't take kindly to me at that first table—or ever, actually. But that was okay. I met their chauvinism with a defense strategy that had been honed throughout my twenty-six years of life: I was obnoxious to them. Unlike that older woman at the other table who was defusing animosity with good-natured jokes (which, I must say, is a strategy I have since adopted, with great results), I was resorting to vocabulary choices designed to make them feel inferior and inadequate. Whenever I pulled in a pot I would gloat in a so-there-look-who's-better-at-this-game-than-whom manner. I wasn't engaged in the camaraderie that I have since learned is common in poker. But because I was keeping myself at a distance, I also was better able to conceal my emotions, to not let on that I had a pair of aces in my hand or that I was bluffing with 8-2 unsuited.

And it also gave me ample ground to observe them, and I could tell that these men were playing a hyperaggressive game around me. They would call when they should have folded. They would raise when they should have called. So deep was the resolve not to let a woman beat them at a game that was so tightly identified with their manhood, they would make the sorts of blundered decisions that were relatively easy to exploit. I could get them unhinged, enticing them into a pot with a subtle "are you really going to let a girl beat you at this?" expression on my face.

It was great.

And then I would smile as the dealer pushed the pile of chips in my direction.

If I learned anything about poker in my baptism at the Crystal Lounge, it's that women, for the most part, have a distinct advantage over men at the table. This has nothing to do with a woman's superior mind or her intuitive nature or her multitasking skills (although these are all formidable strengths at the poker table). It has to do with the mere fact that men sometimes get unhinged in our presence. Even with women they know they have no chance of ever coaxing into the sack, some—not all, but some—forget that poker is a cold, ruthless game of skill and math, in which the strategy should be aimed at winning money from one's opponent. For too many men, the table strategy is aimed at another objective, either luring us back to their apartment for some variant of strip poker or kicking us out of their all-male sanctum. And they may not even be aware of it.

There are two types of guys a woman is likely to encounter at the table. First, there's the flirter. These guys see women as potential sexual partners rather than as formidable poker opponents. They spend less time trying to determine our card holdings than they spend estimating our bra-cup sizes. They flirt. If you don't mind playing along, you should flirt right back at them. Make them feel as if they actually have a chance, and you'll get bets saved in return.

A guy who wants to take you out for Jack and Cokes and some bouncy-bouncy isn't likely to want to take your money. It would get in the way of his real objective. So you'll find they will often not raise you when they should. They will back off from putting the kind of pressure (betting pressure, that is) on you that they would be exerting if you were a guy. They won't bluff as frequently as they otherwise might. And if you're truly lucky, you might actually find them going so far as to tell you when you are beat. In those early days at the Crystal Lounge, I had guys say things like, "Honey, don't call. I have a flush." And they would even show me the cards.

Trust me, they didn't get lucky after the game. But I did walk away with their cash.

Then there's the angry chauvinist. These are guys who get bent out of shape because they've come out for their Wednesday poker night to get away from women, only to find one sitting among them. They see you as someone whose goal in life is to ruin their good time.

If you feel comfortable with the approach, you can unhinge them by antagonizing them. To emphasize your femininity, giggle girlishly when you win pots. Check-raise them at every opportunity. Show them your bluffs. They already don't like you. Why not completely piss them off?

You'll get extra bets from them. This type of man doesn't

want a *girl* to beat him. In an effort to show you who the stronger gender is, these guys will bluff you far too frequently. They will call you too often. Take advantage by calling them down more often than you would another opponent. Make no mistake about it: these guys are trying to bluff you much more than they should be. All those extra bets and extra bluffs that you call down will pay off on the river.

Men: Pay attention. You might mindlessly be giving us your money.

Women: Don't fight such behavior. Use it for the clear edge—and profit—it offers.

It worked for me.

That's how it went my first night at the Crystal Lounge. Ben came back from the bookstore and picked up an empty seat at the other table. He wasn't very good at poker, but the other folks loved him. On the other hand, I wasn't making any friends, but I was watching my chip stack grow. By the time they closed the poker room at two a.m., the drinking-to-extremes construction worker had stumbled out on the arm of his girlfriend, who had spent the better part of an hour leaning against the paneled wall and pleading, "Come on, Rich. Come on. Let's go home. I mean it. Let's go home." I think she even scratched her crotch. A few night-shift workers from the local television station strolled in for maybe half an hour of blowing off some after-work steam. When it was time for us to leave I carried my chips to the cash window, where the tall, balding gentleman counted them out and then slid $168 my way.

Over the course of five hours I had made $118. According to my quick calculations, that came to $23.60 per hour.

Not a high rate of pay for someone who had spent the previous twenty-one years getting the finest education money could buy. But do you know how great it feels to earn enough money to cover the monthly mortgage in one evening?

I put my arm around Ben's waist as we strolled out of the Crystal Lounge. The wind was blowing in the unfortunate direction, bringing with it that smell of a refinery or cow shit. And you know what? I didn't mind. I fingered the twenties and tens in my back pocket and, suddenly, my future didn't look so scary.

17

Monday, May 10, 2004
5:04 P.M.

I'M IN A POT with Ray Bonavida. I have A-A-2-5. It's a huge hand with high and low potential.

I bet $5,000. He raises it to $10,000. I reraise to $15,000. He calls.

And the board comes 3-4-10. I have a pair of aces and a wheel draw.

I bet on the flop and he calls. That gets the pot to $53,000.

I bet on the turn and he raises. I reraise him. He calls. Now the pot is $113,000.

Then I make a wheel on the river, which I don't actually need. In fact, I think the wheel might hurt me because there is the possibility that he might also have a wheel.

I bet $10,000 and he calls. I turn over my hand. He had aces with the bad low. I had aces with the wheel. I scoop the pot.

The $63,000 in chips I win from him knock him down to a stack of $15,000. It pushes me up to about $260,000. I definitely solidify my lead. Erik's behind me, with $140,000. Ron Graham's at $50,000, and Ray Bonavida's at $15,000.

It's Erik who finishes Ray off. Erik flops aces and 9s and Ray misses a flush draw. He shakes hands with each of us and leaves Benny's Bullpen, winning $30,140.

Down to three.

I'm left competing with Erik, one of my best friends and the person who backs me in tournaments like this one, and Ron Graham, a solid player whose habit of remaining quiet at the table can be a bit disarming for a person like me—that is, someone whose mouth rarely stops moving.

I'm chip leader by a substantial margin. But I know that isn't something I can count on for long. If there's one thing that I can predict, it's that the final hours of a poker table can be anything but predictable. I've seen too many tournaments where stacks of chips move back and forth across a final table.

Last night Erik and I talked about how great it would be to go heads-up at the final table. But if that were to happen, did I *really* want it to be him who might knock me out of this tournament in second place? Or what if it were *me* who knocked *him* out? I thought about that for a moment: the idea of possibly knocking out my brother *and* one of my closest friends gave me pause. And then there was Ron Graham, this easygoing guy who had a way of blending into the background. There was something a bit intimidating about that.

You can drown in still waters.

18

I TOLD HOWARD about my winning night at the Crystal Lounge, and a few days later I received from him a package containing several poker books, including David Sklansky's *The Theory of Poker* and Doyle Brunson's *Super/System*. There was something else, too: a check for $2,400 that would comprise my poker bankroll. My brother told me that he had seen something impressive in the way I had been playing poker in Las Vegas during our month there—-he liked my aggressive instincts—and said he was willing to back me as I sharpened my game. I immediately walked to the drugstore and bought a notebook to keep track of my poker activity.

Keeping a record allows you to trace your progress—to learn, for example, the fundamental fact of whether you're a winner or a loser over the long term. Your stats will go a long way in helping you decide when to advance to a higher-limit game, and when to step back.

You also will be able to pick up on subtle patterns in your

play. In addition to recording the hours you play and how much you win or lose, you should indicate mistakes you make each time you play. You'll be amazed at how quickly patterns and lessons emerge. You may discover that you play far too loosely with certain friends, or that you tend to slack off in the sessions following a big winning night.

There are a host of common mistakes people make when they start playing poker. They play too high. They play with competition that's too tough. They play too many hands. They play too passively—they simply call when they could raise. Or they play too long. How do you know when it's time to quit? I never suggest putting an arbitrary time limit on your play, but

Chart your progress in a notebook.

One big mistake people make when they first start playing is that they don't realize how much there is to poker. Obviously, if you're just a recreational player who is out to have fun, there's no need to tackle poker as if it were a course in calculus or macroeconomics. But if you want to make money, you have to take the game seriously. You have to read books. You have to put in the hours. You have to discuss poker with other people. And you have to keep a record of your wins and losses. Money is the measure for keeping score, and if you're serious about improving your poker skills, you have to be fairly disciplined about this, even if your poker is limited to a Wednesday-night game with friends.

Never lose more than thirty big bets. That's about the most you can expect to win on a very good night.

I do believe in putting a limit on the amount you should lose in a day: thirty bets.

Unless you truly become a student of the game, you're not likely to become good. Let me rephrase that. You might actually become good, but it is going to take you a very, very long time.

So for the next two days I did nothing but read those books and phone Howard about every other hour and assault him with questions. Then I got back into the Honda with Ben and made the trip to Billings with my bankroll. This time, I wanted to play in the higher-stakes game, the $10-$20 game. The players were a regular succession of boisterous cowboys and grizzled retirees wagering their disability checks. We played in the depressing basement.

Some of the guys took kindly to me. Kannon Richards was a gentle man who was hunched over with age and used to give me bags of bulbs to plant. There were a few other friendly folks, as well. John Merino had trouble controlling his temper, which taught me the dangers of blowing up at the table, and Linda Gallagher, his girlfriend at the time, was a dealer who helped me feel comfortable at the table. John Louden, the best player in the game, gave me advice on picking up on people's betting patterns. Dwight Gauger was a regular player who was losing his sight to glaucoma—I helped him decorate his apartment. There was a fellow named Bob Bradbook, a rancher from Rapelje, which is dry land for ranching, who was big and had gaps in his teeth and was perpetually jolly; give him a white beard and an apple-red suit and he would make a perfect Santa Claus.

At the Crystal Lounge, I found myself becoming more open to being with different kinds of people. Frankly, growing up, I was taught to think that only educated people—people smarter or more accomplished than me—deserved my respect, that if you didn't go to a top college, you weren't worth talking to. I came to realize that this was just unfair, that you need to take people for who they are. And they can often teach you some pretty amazing things.

Letting go of preconceived judgments not only made me a better person, it made me a better poker player. Judge somebody and you're seeing what you think is there, not what's really there, and this bias skews your read on them at the poker table. You'll lose at poker. More important, you'll lose at life.

So, I was making some new friends, but not everyone was welcoming. I'd learned at an early age how to survive among people who were a lot different from me. But just as I secretly wanted my classmates at St. Paul's to find me pretty, and funny, and smart, and thin, and worthy of their friendship, I would have preferred a more uniformly congenial environment in Billings as I honed my poker skills. I was having no trouble making friends in Columbus. I felt comfortable around folks who were working hard and dedicated to building strong families, and who took the time to be friendly to strangers and to one another. But then I would drive to the Crystal Lounge and sometimes feel as if I had landed right back in high school.

One night when I was losing, a fellow wearing a Raiders cap announced to the table, "She can just go across the street to the Radisson Hotel and put her legs up in the air and win it back." Ordinarily, I would either ignore guys who were so offensive or shove it right back at them. In that case, however, I was floored. Adrenaline pumped through my body. Ben came over and threatened to flatten the guy. It did the trick.

There were a lot of hard-core gambling addicts in the game. One of them was a Greek man who was a manager at the Radisson. Each night he arrived with buckets of money, and I never figured out where he got his bankroll—until one day he disappeared, and word came that he had been embezzling from the hotel. There was a gentle man with a flock of kids, a gambling addict who had been through the program at Rimrock, the local rehabilitation center. Apparently he had done so well that he was kept on as a counselor. Then one day he sat down at the Crystal and started playing again. He ended up kiting checks and losing his job. Indebted to the owner of the Crystal Lounge, he started dealing the game.

I was learning what poker could do to people.

My new schedule was this: I would arrive at the Crystal Lounge in the afternoon, when the tight players were in abundance. I found it a lot easier to run a game over when the players were more conservative. That atmosphere typically changed by around eight p.m. At night, players tended to be on the wild side, raising and reraising to the point where the pot would reach the state-mandated $300 limit even before any cards were flopped.

As I picked up the subtleties of poker in that first month, I lost on a fairly regular basis. Some nights we'd actually drive home with a surplus, but many nights we'd head down I-90 with a loss. Ben was having trouble keeping busy while I played until the two a.m. closing, by which time the bookstore and record store and other places he would visit to occupy himself had long closed. More often than not, we would argue on the ride home. Then, back in Columbus, I would carefully write down a chronology of my poker activity. After that I would phone Howard to go over the hands I had played to learn if I played the right hands—and if I did, if I had played them correctly.

Ben didn't see the big picture. I remember him saying, "Your little hobby is costing us money."

At one point, I was actually about to agree with him. I had lost most of the original $2,400 that Howard had fronted me. I had run out of chips for the night and had no cash on hand, so I wrote a check for $300 to the Crystal Lounge. That night, I got lucky. In hand after hand, I was able to regain my losses, amid increasingly hostile opponents.

By the end of the month, I tallied my winnings. I looked at the numbers I had written on the page. In my first month I had won $2,860. It was a revelation.

After I told Howard, he made me an official proposal: he would stake me in exchange for 50 percent of my winnings. I think Howard saw a spark in the questions I'd asked, and in the way I'd quickly taken to the game.

And he was right: at the end of that first year, I had made $15,000—keeping $7,500 of it for myself and giving Howard his share. At that point, I never thought I would become a professional poker player. It was just something I was doing to make money. We were able to graduate from our near-constant diet of Ramen noodles. We were able to pay our mortgage, and to keep up the insurance payments on the Honda.

Poker was the way we paid the bills, got by. But it wasn't a career.

Howard relocated to Las Vegas that year. It's not an uncommon move for a professional gambler. But in his case, there was another factor involved. He ran a major sports-betting operation in New York, which was raided during one of Mayor Rudolph Giuliani's crusades against gambling. Everybody was thrown into the Tombs for a few days, including my mom's boyfriend Dale, who worked with Howard at the time. So Howard moved to Las Vegas, where the atmosphere was more favorable for sports betting.

In January of 1994, Howard phoned and suggested I try my hand again in Las Vegas, where there always seemed to be a tournament of some level to play in. The Arctic wind in Montana hadn't stopped blowing since Halloween and the snow was leaking through our flimsy roof. It made perfect sense to flee the weather for Vegas and play in satellites, where a small entry fee, courtesy of my brother, gave me the chance to win a seat in big tournaments. Ben stayed home.

I was in Vegas for three weeks, competing in satellites and doing well—making my way into a few tournaments. The separation wasn't great for my marriage. At one point, I was talking to Ben long-distance from a phone in the Four Queens Casino, and we started screaming at each other about when I would be coming home. A sports-betting business associate of my brother's was standing nearby, and after the conversation was over, he offered to make a bet on how long my marriage would last. He put the over-under on our marriage at two years, and we bet $500, which at the time was a fortune for me. (The deal: if the marriage lasted until 1996, I collected on the bet. It did, and I did.)

A few months later, Ben and I drove back down to Vegas for the World Series of Poker. We lived in the Golden Nugget for a month, compliments of Howard. Along with six hundred other contenders, I entered the first event, the $1,500 Limit Hold 'em Tournament. I was nervous about playing with such a huge field of competitors. Very early on, I almost got knocked out, but then I won a huge pot with jacks. From that point, I played fairly aggressively. We eventually got down to two tables and I ended up coming in fourteenth, which won me $7,230. It was the World Series of Poker's twenty-fifth anniversary year, so everybody who ended up in the money was given a commemorative silver nugget. Somebody stole mine the very night I won it. I remember being in tears, going up to Jim Albrecht, who ran the tournament, and pleading for another silver nugget on the grounds that I was never going to end up in the money at another World Series event in my life. Albrecht, who died a few years ago, handed me another silver nugget just as Howard said: "Now, why don't you play in the satellite for the twenty-five-hundred-dollar Limit Hold 'em tournament?"

So I won a seat at that tournament. I was fine at first, and found myself winning more pots than I was losing. But as more people got knocked out, as we got down to fewer people, I could feel myself growing increasingly anxious—it felt like a terrible buzz saw was working its way through my insides. I was nervous about the money.

Ultimately, we got down to a final table. Accustomed to holding my feelings in my stomach, I felt the dam crumble. I needed to throw up. So I raced to the women's room just moments before we were to start playing and puked. Then, maybe sixty seconds later, on the way back to the final table, I needed to throw up again. There was a trash can in the hallway, and I just leaned over and hurled, while railbirds and players watched.

"Isn't that Howard Lederer's sister?" I heard someone say.

I was new at this, and not sure it was the right thing for me to be doing. I was too young and too inexperienced, too freaked out about the money. I walked over to the gift shop and bought a bottle of Pepto-Bismol and placed it right in front of me on the green felt surface of the final table.

It occurred to me that I was in awful pain and suffering those panic and anxiety attacks only when the poker action stopped. I felt fine when we were actually playing, and I could even play well—possibly as a way of beating back those terrible feelings of anxiety. (One of the first things you learn in cognitive therapy is that one of the best ways to get out of panic mode is to be distracted. Poker was my distraction.)

I wound up in fifth place—not bad for my second open tournament. For those two days of work, I won $28,500. That was more than our entire budget for the previous two years combined. Now there was buzz about this chick, Howard's little sister, who was winning at the table. And people like Erik Seidel, T. J. Cloutier, and Steve Zolotov were really nice to me. I'll never forget that.

Finally, my brother told me I should play in the final event, which began on Monday, May 9. The final event is no-limit and I had never played that version of poker before, so Howard suggested I play in some multitable super-satellites for the chance at winning a seat at that event. I won a seat right away, and then continued playing in more of the satellites to get some no-limit practice. I did it, and added $3,500 to my winnings.

On the first day of the final event, I got drawn to my brother's table. This was before they made the rule disallowing relatives from playing at the same table, other than at the final table. I had $14,000 in chips and opened the pot for $800 with a pair of aces. The bet came around to Howard and he had only $6,000 in chips. He moved in. I obviously called with aces.

He had A-K.

I knocked him out. Poker is my brother's life, and it had been his dream to win this event. It felt like a horrible fluke. He didn't act too devastated, but I resorted to tears. I'm fairly certain this was a World Series of Poker first: watching some girl crying because she knocked out her brother. Humberto Brenes, a big and charming player from Costa Rica who hardly

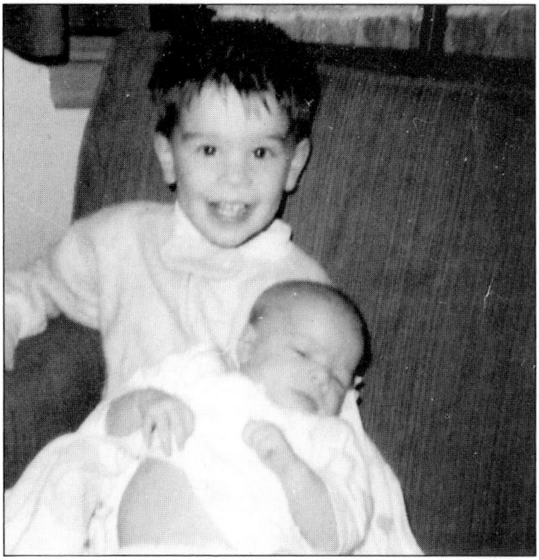

1. The first picture of Howard and me together. He's smiling because he finally has someone he can beat at cards.

2. Even as an infant I had a knack for fashion.

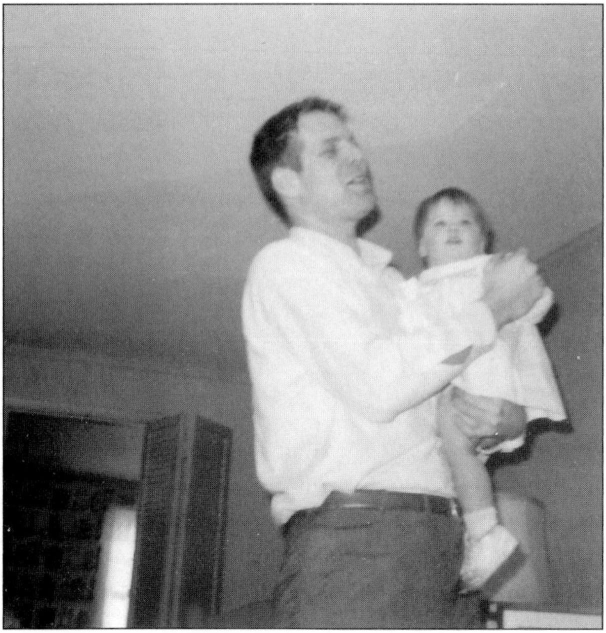

3. Father and daughter—my first dance lesson.

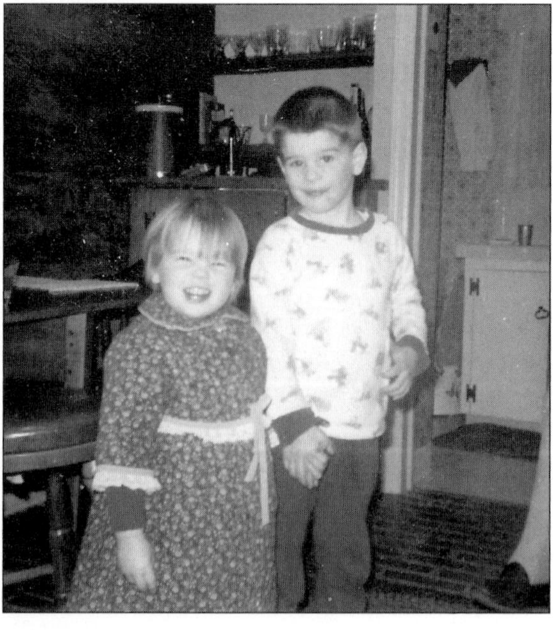

4. Howard and me: pre-poker faces.

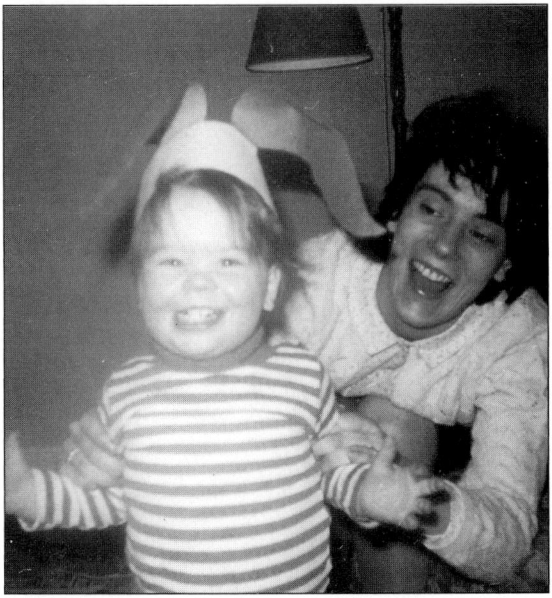

5. Mom and me. What's up with the hat?

6. I gave up pigtails shortly after this photo was taken.

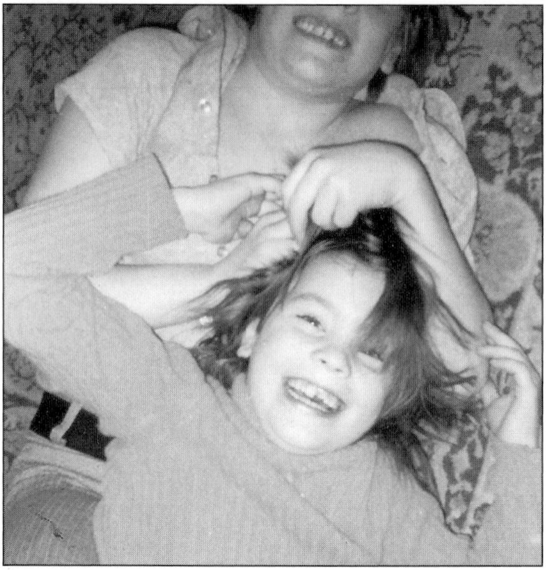

7. Howard torturing me when I was eight. I get back at him when I can in tournaments.

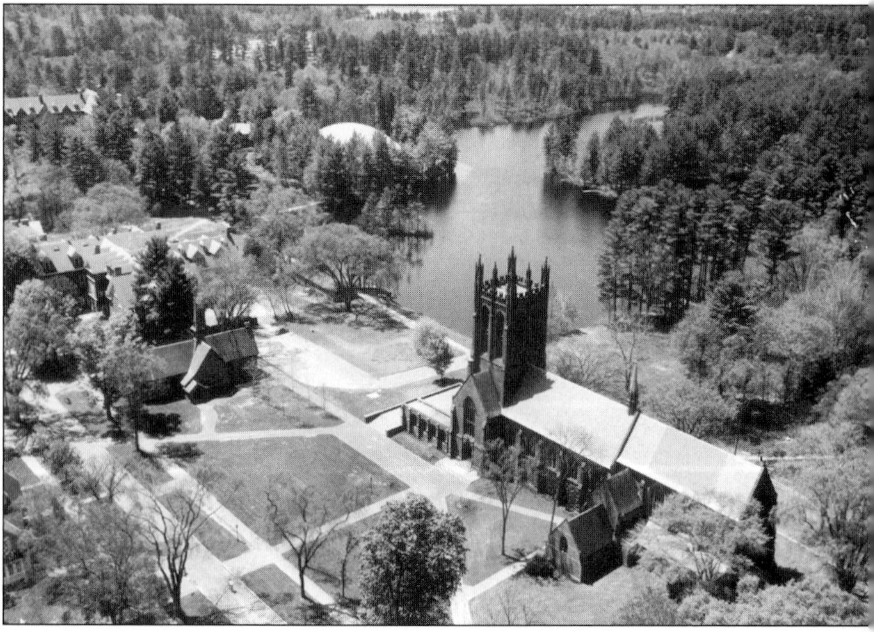

8. St. Paul's School in the 1970s—although it could be the 1870s.

9. Sophomore year at Columbia. In a rare break from clubbing, I'm hanging out with friends at a park in upstate New York.

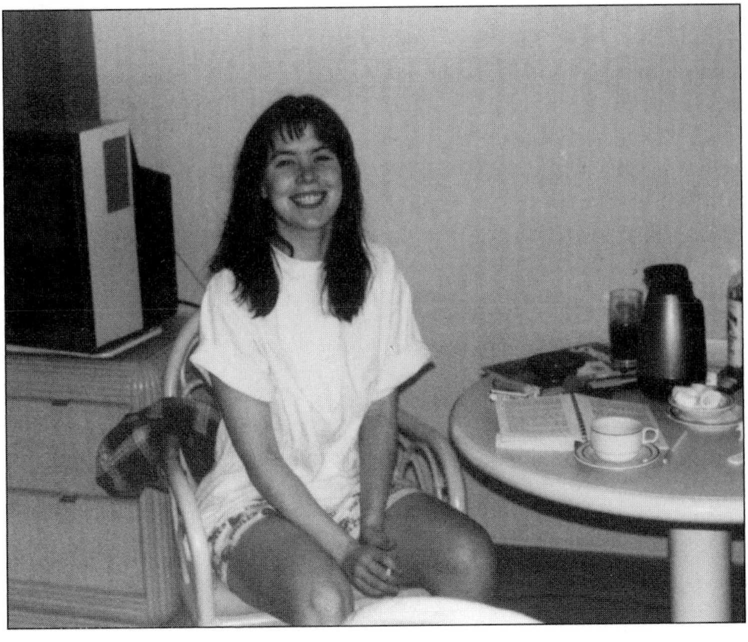

10. That's me at the Golden Nugget in 1991. I was still in grad school at Penn and it was my first trip to Las Vegas. . . .

11. University of Pennsylvania's Psychology Department took pictures of all incoming grad students to hang on the wall.

12. With my sister Katy, the poet, during a visit to Renee's house in the Bay Area in 1991. Katy was a student at UC Berkeley.

13. At my wedding rehearsal with my dad. He still wears that tie.

14. Ben and me at our "leap" wedding on February 29, 1992, at Grandma Betty's house in Darien, Connecticut. What panic disorder?

15. The blushing bride.

16. Celebrating our nuptials: Pony Duke, Ben's father (with his trademark handlebar mustache); Mary Ellen Duke, Ben's stepmom; and that's Ambassador Andrew Biddle Duke, Ben's grandfather, on the right.

17. The Crystal Lounge in downtown Billings—epicenter of Montana's poker action.

18. Just a wholesome storefront in Big Sky country.

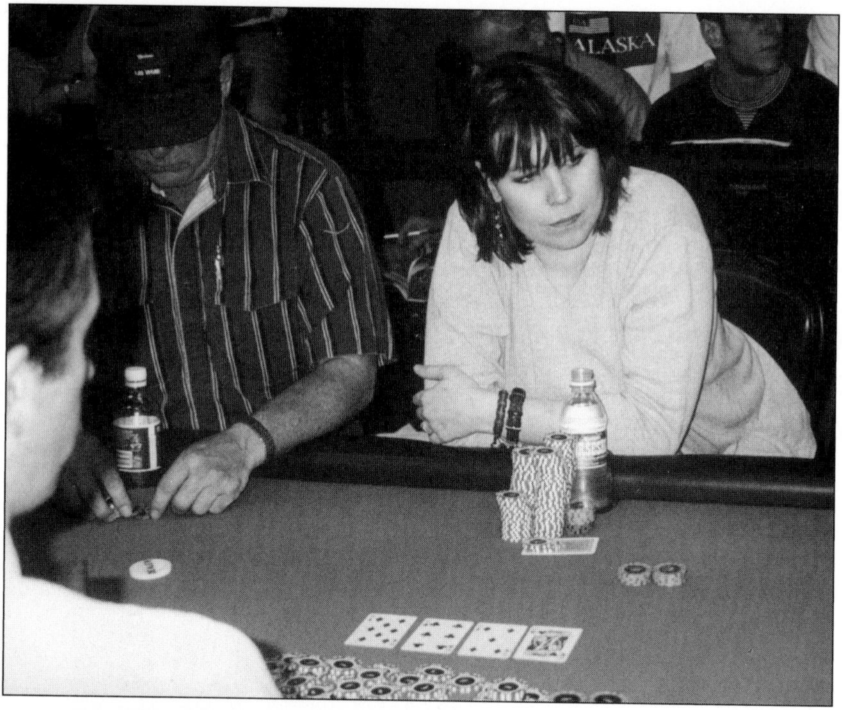

19. Pregnant and feeling it at the 2000 World Series of Poker Main Event. Weeks before giving birth to Lucy.

20. A final table of the 2003 World Series of Poker. I made two final tables that year. The $2,500 Omaha Hi-Lo Split (I placed sixth) and the $1,500 Limit Hold 'em Shootout (second).

21. The 2003 World Series of Poker Main Event.

22. The 2004 World Series of Poker $2,000 Omaha Hi-Lo Split Event.

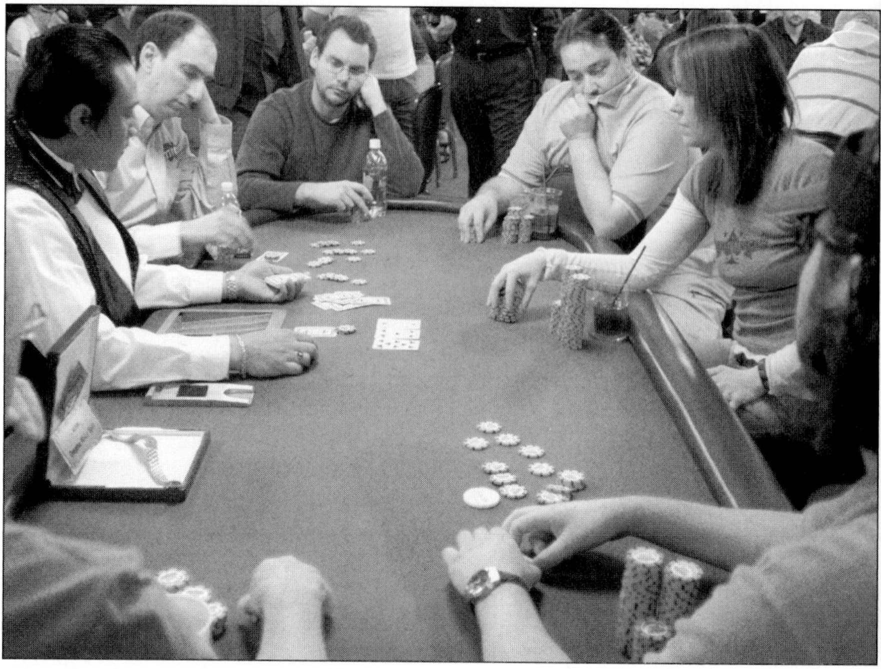

23. A final table of the 2004 World Series of Poker $2,000 Omaha Hi-Lo Split. To the dealer's left you see Erik Seidel, Don McNamara, Todd Brunson, and me. Partially visible are Ron Graham (left) and Ray Bonavida (right).

24. Crushing Howard's back after my bracelet win at the 2004 World Series of Poker $2,000 Omaha Hi-Lo Split Event.

25. Miss America cries—so can I.

26. Feeling like a champ after winning my World Series of Poker bracelet!

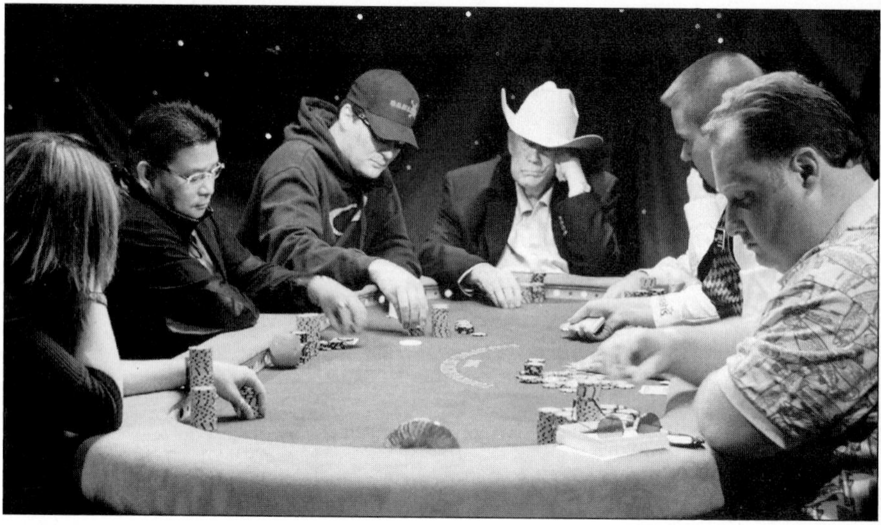

27. The first-ever World Series of Poker Tournament of Champions in September 2004. It dawned on me that with the ten best players in the world, nobody would make any mistakes.

28. At the World Series of Poker Tournament of Champions: the only female among nine men.

29. Strong chip position at the World Series of Poker Tournament of Champions.

30. Heads-up with Phil Hellmuth at the World Series of Poker Tournament of Champions, within grasp of the $2 million prize. Hey Phil, if you think I'm bluffing, why don't you just call?

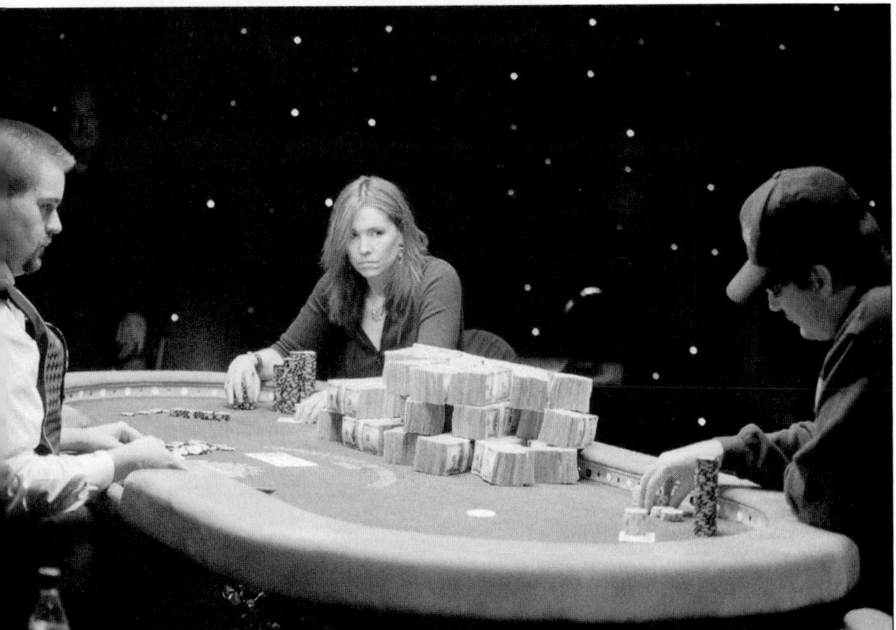

31. Will my psychology work on Phil?

32. Me and my $2 million at the World Series of Poker Tournament of Champions. Exhausted but rich.

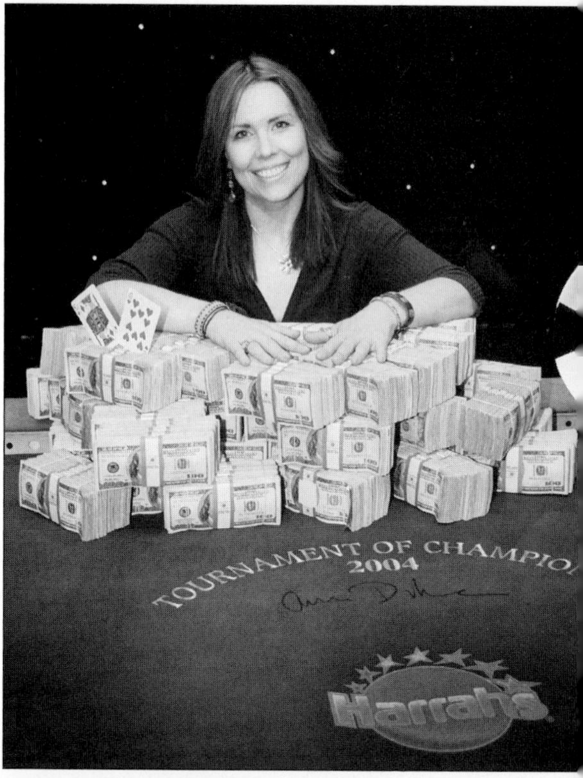

33. The real treasures of my life: Nelly, Lucy, Leo, and Maud.

spoke English, comforted me. He just got up and hugged me. It was the first time I met him and he seemed to fully understand how rough it was for me.

So I ended that first day with more than $30,000 in chips, which put me thirty-fifth in chip position.

The morning of the second day of the most important poker tournament known to humankind, I was trapped in my hotel room with the dry heaves. It was vile. I couldn't eat. I couldn't keep anything down. I was just freaking out. Out of the 268 participants who entered the tournament, only thirty-four had more chips than I did. I finally got it together enough to leave my hotel room and walk across the Fremont Street mall to Binion's Horseshoe, which by then had become as familiar to me as my own living room in Montana. A pair of reporters approached me—all of a sudden, I was somebody who journalists wanted to interview. My body convulsed with the dry heaves. At least I didn't puke on the press.

I made it through the day.

That first day, I was just trying to stay in the game. By the second day, the game had started to reveal itself to me. I began to understand the power of the chips, and the power of people's perceptions. I bluffed with a nine-high flush draw against an ace-high flush draw. We got down to four tables and, amazing as it seems, I'd become the chip leader, with $95,000 in chips. You have to make it down to three tables to get in the money. I opened the pot on the button with $5,000. I held a pair of kings. My opponent, whom I didn't know, moved all-in for $65,000 out of the big blind, drastically overbetting the pot. He could have reraised to $25,000 and found the exact same information—that I had him beat. He didn't have to put all his chips at risk. I thought about it for about a second and tossed in the $60,000 to call him.

He had A-3 (offsuit).

I had two kings. I was the 2-to-1 favorite to win. This was the final event of the World Series. . . .

And in the long tradition of being pummeled by someone else's bad play, the first card off the deck was an ace.

His pair of aces knocked me down to $30,000.

Wounded, I still managed to limp into the final three tables with $27,000 in chips.

Learn as many games as you can.

Work on becoming a really good poker player, as opposed to becoming a good Seven-Card Stud player, a good Hold 'em player, or a good Omaha 8-or-Better player. Because all the games pose different mathematical problems. As you learn different games, you become a better player, overall. It forces you to understand poker theory, which can be applied to any of the games.

I started playing Limit Hold 'em, and I eventually found my way into the $400-$800 Limit Hold 'em game. Meanwhile I played in the $15-$30 Stud game. It took me a year of playing Stud to work my way up to where I could play $75-$150. Omaha 8-or-Better was a game I just took to immediately. It was a good fit for me, so I never stepped back in level.

Play ended for the day; we were to return the next day at noon.

That morning, I woke up without any trace of nervousness. I figured I had no chance to win. Indeed, I ended up coming in twenty-eighth. That was still in the money, and I got $18,000. But I couldn't shake the heartbreaking loss—I still can't.

By the time Ben and I were checking out of the Golden Nugget for the drive up to Montana, I had won a total of $57,000 for my month of poker playing. After settling up with my brother and his partner, who had also staked some of my play, I ended up with about $20,000 in cash.

Not bad for a novice.

With these winnings in mind, Howard encouraged me to play professionally, and urged Ben and me to move to Las Vegas. It wasn't Ben's first choice of a place to live, but it would enable me to start a career. Besides, neither of us figured we'd live there over the long haul. Howard found us a house in a transitional neighborhood on the east side of town, and more than three times the size of our house in Montana. Plus, it had hot water. Howard held the mortgage and we just had to pay him.

Ben and I drove back to Columbus. I took half the cash I had earned and bought a few rental properties in Columbus and fixed them up. We used some of the remaining money for our move. We packed up our belongings—including the cartons containing my Ph.D. research—and rented a van, and off we went.

No longer would I play poker merely to help make ends meet. I would become a professional. I was beginning to admit to myself that it was . . . fun. I could talk about hands for hours with Howard; I had never been as charged up by psycholinguistics. Or anything else, for that matter. I started getting to know other players, and I liked their spirit. I liked the diversity, too. I liked the gray-skinned older guys who learned the game in back alleys and were sharper and more astute than most Ivy Leaguers. I liked the fun-loving younger guys in their early twenties who were as enthusiastic about winning a hand with an overpair as any five-year-old catching his first fish. I liked the polite and earnest folks who spent as much time rehearsing with their church choir as they did practicing at poker tables. Everyone, it seemed, was optimistic—and the poker table was the meeting ground.

Ultimately, you have to be an optimist to play this game. I was inspired by my success in the World Series of Poker and by Howard's unwavering confidence in me. And, of course, I was anxious about the changing course my life was about to take.

We steered the U-Haul out of Columbus and headed west on Interstate 90, not knowing at the time that I was six weeks pregnant.

19

Monday, May 10, 2004
8:12 P.M.

ERIK AND RON WANT to make a deal. Because the difference between the second-place winner (who would receive $75,780) and the third-place winner (who would get $38,740) is so substantial (okay, for the math challenged, it amounts to more than $37,000), these guys want to hedge their bets. They want to agree to a deal in which each of them would take a percentage of what the other won. Basically, whoever finishes higher will give the other person $12,000.

They haven't asked me to participate because I have such a huge chip advantage over both of them that it wouldn't be in my best interest to take part in the deal. But they ask my permission because it's usually not the case that you would allow two people to make a deal and not include the third.

Ordinarily, such a two-sided deal would work to my disadvantage—each player could play soft against the other, effectively colluding against me. But Erik's a good friend and I know he's not going to cheat me. And Ron seems like a person of integrity.

Actually, deals like this are made all the time. Generally, they're done to allow competitors at the final table to hedge their bets. If you want to make a deal, you say to a tournament official, "Can we take some time?" and then they stop the clock and you go out and talk to the other person.

Once you've agreed to an arrangement, you tell the tournament director the details of the deal so that it can be enforced. Long ago, there were cases in which a deal had been struck and then somebody reneged. To prevent such abuses, the tournament director writes down the details and everybody agrees to the terms before you start playing again. This is not cheating, by the way; it's just a way to accommodate for how tournament poker is structured. Not only are there huge differences between the top spots, but also, when the blinds get high, they create a high-variance situation. So you want to lock up your equity and decrease your variance whenever you can.

Speaking of deals, Chris Ferguson and I have a great arrangement. We had already known each other for a few years when we found ourselves playing at the same table—the next-to-final table—in the championship event of the 2000 World Series. I was still pregnant with Lucy and feeling miserable. We were at Level Fifteen. The ante was $3,000. The blinds were $15,000 and $30,000.

I had $300,000 in chips. He had about the same. Like many pros in such situations, we decided to hedge our bets, so to speak. We made a deal. We would trade 5 percent. He would give me 5 percent of what he ultimately won, and I would give him 5 percent of what I won.

At one point, with A-9 in my hand, I raised all-in. Chris called, turning over pocket aces. Chris's aces knocked me out of the World Series in tenth place. I cashed out with $52,260. But he went on to win first place, and $2.5 million. And, as agreed, he gave me 5 percent. (For the math challenged, that's $125,000.) We became fast friends, and we've been trading 5 percent ever since. He's always telling me, "I knocked you out, so I owe you." Occasionally I'll go up to him and say, "Are you sure you don't want to get off that trade?" He always has the same response: "I can't get off that trade for life because I knocked you out," he says. He's so honorable.

While I didn't want to deny Erik and Ron their deal, I would later learn that my brother had an opposing view. So did my friend Paul Wolfe, who traveled to Vegas from his home in Florida. Both would later tell me they felt strongly that I didn't have anything to gain from it. I call it a deposit in the Bank of Karma.

Back at the table, I'm happy to let the short stacks battle it out.

In tournaments, if you've got a solid chip position, it becomes mathematically correct to stay out of pots and let the short stacks knock each other out.

Their chips are of relatively equal value against each other. Meanwhile, the short stacks often try to avoid the big stacks because they know that the big stack can break them. So the rule is: if a short stack is willing to tangle with you, it often means that they have a pretty good holding.

At our three-handed final table, that's what Ron is doing. He is playing in a style that is likely to get him second in the tournament. Erik, on the other hand, is trying hard to win. He's playing looser and, as a result, is more likely to end up in either first or third place. But he keeps butting up against me.

There's an irony to the fact that, as I enjoy my dominant chip position status, Erik and Ron are battling it out for second place. The two had grappled in a similar situation at the final table of the 1988 World Series of Poker main event. Erik busted Ron, who went out in third place. Erik then lost to Johnny Chan in the final hand that was immortalized on celluloid in the movie *Rounders*.

This time around, though, I'm not certain that Erik, with his loose playing—which is the correct way to be playing, in my opinion—will emerge victorious.

We now stand as follows: me, $334,000; Erik Seidel, $65,000; Ron Graham, $65,000.

When we are three-handed I beat Erik out of every pot. There is one hand where I raise before the flop. I have K-K-7-7 and the board comes 7-7-5.

Erik bets.

I raise.

He folds.

"Oh, I flopped the nuts with two pair," I joke as I add his chips to my stack.

Several hands later, I raise with A-3-4-6. The board comes 2-5-Q. Erik pushes in his few remaining chips. He turns over A-9-7-10. But I get a wheel on the turn. My good friend is out.

He looks disappointed—not devastated—as we hug. "I'm sorry

it was you. I would have loved to have played heads-up like we talked about last night," I say.

"I got a few split pots against her," he tells a reporter as he nears the door. "But I just couldn't make the best hand against her."

Now I turn to Ron Graham, the man who stands in the way of my first World Series bracelet. He's not very demonstrative—and as a result, very difficult to read. He is also proving to be a solid Omaha player. But I have amassed about eight times as many chips as he has, piled high in tall towers (I've got $440,000 and he has $52,000). Still, if I've learned anything about poker in all these years, it's this: I'd be a fool to assume that bracelet was already mine.

20

I ALWAYS THOUGHT I would be too selfish for motherhood, but Ben was really eager to become a father. On the other hand, I wanted to move to Las Vegas and Ben didn't. It's not as if I'm a big fan of Las Vegas; I'm not. And I didn't think it would be a healthy environment in which to raise kids. But I was making a living at poker. Ben kept trying to make deals—like we would move to Vegas for five years and then move back to Montana. We both wanted the marriage to work, so we each gave what the other wanted. Marriage is all about compromise, right? We agreed to give Vegas five years.

We spent the latter half of 1994 and the first few months of 1995 getting accustomed to our new home, our new city, and the fact that we were going to be parents. When we moved to Vegas, one of the first things I tackled at my brother's behest was learning other games. I was trying to learn Stud so I started playing in the $15-$30 Stud games. I worked my way up for an entire year, while I was also sitting down at the $400-$800 Hold 'em game. I played in some no-limit tournaments, but there weren't a lot of them happening on a regular basis, so I just really focused on limit poker, and on expanding the games I could play.

At the time, the Mirage was the epicenter for poker. I would play in the $50-$100 game there, and generally won between $50 and $100 an hour. I was seven months pregnant when I played in something called the Binion's Hall of Fame Tournament, and I placed fifth—winning $35,000. When I think about this part of my pregnancy with Maud, I remember the overwhelming heartburn that never quit. But I kept on competing until I was nine months pregnant and too big to play. Then I waited at home, without poker to distract me.

I had already decided to have the baby at home. I told people that it was because it would be better for the baby. But the fact is, I was terrified of the hospitals and the doctors and the sterile environment.

Then it happened. At the three-weeks-before-due-date point, I started feeling a terrible pressure on my stomach, and was suddenly having trouble keeping anything down.

As somebody who had previously expressed anxiety through her digestive system, I immediately became anxious about my inability to keep food down, which, of course, only made things worse. Like many first-time moms, I had been a little bit nervous to start with. The stomach problems just intensified those feelings. It was horrible, and I ended up spending the last three weeks of my pregnancy overwhelmed by the sensation of holding back a deluge.

It only got worse when I went into labor. As odd as it sounds, I actually started panicking about the responsibility of raising a child. It was dawning on me that it would be a huge change in my life (well, duh). And truly, I had no idea how I was going to handle it. I started having anxiety attacks in tandem with the onset of labor.

As planned, I phoned Renee, who, over the years, has remained my closest friend, and who had married one of my best friends from college. She had not yet become a midwife but had nonetheless agreed to be on hand for the home birth to help Margie, the midwife I had hired. It was six a.m. on March 7 when I phoned Renee. Her flight from San Francisco landed around noon.

My mom was there to help out with the birth, too, but there wasn't much she could do. And I wasn't doing a great job of handling the contractions. I was anxious. I was dehydrated. It was not pretty. So Margie and Renee arrived while I was sitting on the toilet, with my mom seated in front of me and me digging my fingernails into her shoulders with every contraction, which were accompanied by waves of panic. It all came back to me—every panic attack I had suffered—and it was torture. I was freaking out.

The pushing was nothing compared to the panic—literally, one, two, and there was my beautiful little Maud, named for my maternal great-grandmother.

I couldn't stop looking at her face. She was all mine. I was thrilled. And overwhelmingly scared. Ben was by my side, and seemed happy that we both had come through more or less unscathed.

Renee stayed, with her seven-month-old daughter, Astrid, until the next morning, at which point I was kind of left there with this baby, and I still hadn't gotten over the anxiety. Something awful had kick-started when I went into labor. And it didn't end for the following year and a half. For eighteen long months I endured the same sort of anxiety-depression-panic disorder I had suffered earlier in my life. Then, I had a promising career in academia. Now, I had a beautiful baby. A husband. A promising career in poker. But none of that seemed to make me feel better. And I was rapidly losing weight.

What I learned from this terrible time is that there isn't a lot of support for new moms who aren't feeling happy, although, to be honest, I didn't exert much effort to seek help. And I didn't take any medication. "I'm over panic attacks," I kept saying to myself. "I've already done this. I can do it again." I also felt as if I were *supposed* to be really happy with my baby, and that life was *supposed* to be wonderful, and so I felt the pressure to feel that. I adored Maud, obviously; this was an old problem rearing its ugly head.

Mercifully, after about eighteen months, those feelings subsided on their own. But they weren't far from my mind. Three months after I gave birth to Maud, I played in the 1995 World Series and did surprisingly well. I made four final tables, taking breaks to nurse my infant daughter in the buffet of Binion's Horseshoe Hotel and Casino. I heard whispers of disapproval from other patrons. I was sorry if I made them feel uncomfortable, but the fact is, I had to make a living, and I had a newborn to tend to.

Just as I had decided to supplement my gambling career by investing in Montana real estate early on, I thought another way to diversify would be to start a poker magazine. Along with my brother and a few other backers, I invested $10,000 to launch a new publication. (At the time, this was a huge financial commitment for me.)

I thought the timing was perfect. There wasn't anything like it on the newsstands. It would be called *Poker World*, and we could appeal to professionals and garden-variety fans alike. Vegas casinos seemed to maintain limitless advertising budgets. It all seemed to make sense. I had always done well in writing, and I had access to a few other people with strong editorial skills; both my mother and Katy were now living in Vegas to be near Howard and me. Mom was working for Howard's sports-betting operation, and Katy, having just graduated from UC Berkeley with degrees in English and anthropology, needed a job. She could be hired by the magazine.

Mistake. I was trying to make the magazine work against tremendous odds. For one thing, it wasn't the right time for a poker magazine—that wouldn't happen until 2003, when Barry Shulman, who toiled in Seattle real estate before moving to Las Vegas, made the brilliant move to buy and significantly improve the freebie *Card Player* magazine. Also, I didn't get along with one of the principals involved. I didn't get along with my sister, either. And I didn't have the money to hire the right kind of staff. In fact, none of us knew exactly what we were doing, and I had pretty much taken the whole success or failure of the magazine onto myself.

The truth is, all I really wanted to do was play poker. Nothing's as thrilling to me. Nothing makes me feel as alive, lucky, invincible, and humbled. Nothing is as challenging or gratifying. And while I really thought it was a good idea to try to marry my love of poker with my skill as a writer, I realized I had no idea how to run a magazine, and all this venture did was take time away from my game.

My dip into the chilly editorial waters lasted long enough for us to produce six monthly issues. We created a beautiful magazine. And when we ultimately had to pull the plug, I felt awful—awful for the people who lost money, and for the people who lost their jobs.

It was clear what I had to do: concentrate on poker. It was the only sure way I knew how to support Ben and Maud. And it had a way of reeling me in. Like a lover, the more I learned about poker, the more I was taken with it.

21

Monday, May 10, 2004
9:04 P.M.

FRIENDS ARE GATHERED behind me—Perry Friedman and Paul Wolfe, Chris Ferguson and his girlfriend. Erik left briefly, but has returned to watch most of my heads-up match with Ron Graham. Howard's at a meeting.

As heads-up competitors, Ron and I couldn't be more dissimilar. He's thoughtful, deliberate, almost meditative as he plays his hands, sitting there in his green polo shirt and khaki pants. With his glasses and receding hairline, he looks to be the perfect Anyman—a genial and easygoing bureaucrat from the innards of state government, perhaps. He wears earplugs. Somebody from the press asks if that's to block out all the noise I'm making.

"Probably," he replies, straight-faced.

I'm acting as if I'm still back in the clubs in New York, circa 1984: chipper, talkative, demonstrative, cracking jokes to my friends as I sit there on my bare feet in my jeans and long-sleeve pink top layered with a gray ultimatebet.com T-shirt. And why not feel so upbeat? I'm clearly in the lead in a big way. When we started our two-handed play, I had $410,000 in chips, and Ron had $50,000.

I raise before the flop holding K-J-2-3.

He calls.

The board comes K-J-5.

He bets and I raise. I'm thinking: I flopped top two. It's unlikely he has a hand that can beat me.

He calls.

The turn is a small card—I have a low draw. It'll be very hard for me to get scooped on the pot.

He checks. I bet.

He calls.

The river is a 10. He bets out. I call.

He makes a straight. It's a gut-shot—there were only four cards that could have given him the pot. It's a $50,000 hand and it doubles up his chips, when in fact I should have had him out. I have a brief, torturous flash of unhappiness in which I imagine the worst possible scenario unfolding—namely, that I would blow the eight-to-one lead

Evaluate your winning streak with a critical eye.

When you're winning a lot, determine what's attributable to a good run of cards and what's attributable to doing something different in your game. There's no problem with admitting you had a lucky hand. Winning streaks aren't 100 percent skill and losing streaks aren't 100 percent bad luck.

and slump away a loser. So many times I had made it so close to victory, only to be knocked down in the last possible seconds of the tournament. I catch myself muttering, "Not again" and "Why me?" under my breath.

But I shake it off. I still have more than three times the number of chips Ron has (I have $360,000 to his $100,000).

It's around nine p.m. in the world outside of Benny's Bullpen, and I know my kids are getting ready for bed at Howard's house. By now I know they've heard from Howard that I'm still hanging in there. I hope they're proud of their mom.

22

MOTHERHOOD.

In 1998, the Denver Broncos made it to Super Bowl XXXII. A lifelong Broncos fan, Ben was ecstatic when he landed a pair of tickets to the game. The only problem was that the game was scheduled for January 25 and our second baby was due on January 24.

As we had so many times before, Ben and I made a deal. I told him that if I gave birth before the Super Bowl, he could go. So when January 24 arrived with no signs of labor, I called Margie, who had done such a great job delivering Maud, and asked her to induce me.

Right after Margie broke my water, I started panicking. Obviously, I already had Maud, so it wasn't so much about the responsibility of having a child this time, but more about the fact that I was terrified of the possibility of eighteen months of postpartum depression. But in two short hours, we had little Leo, and Ben took off for the game, which would turn out to be the first Bronco victory in a Super Bowl. They defeated the heavily favored Green Bay Packers 31–24, ending a fourteen-game losing streak for AFC teams in the Super Bowl.

As I had with Maud, I took some time off from poker after Leo was born, which proved essential when Ben and I decided to move back to Montana. (Super Bowl victory or not, he was growing increasingly unhappy in Las Vegas, and we were approaching our five-year deadline, so I agreed.) Inconvenience be damned, I would commute to Vegas to play poker. Montana's better for raising kids. And Ben would feel more at home. At the time, my mom was moving up to Columbus with Dale in order to be closer to her grandchildren, and Katy had already departed for New York to write poetry and work in financial services. My dad had left the cold of New Hampshire for the year-round tennis playing in San Diego with his new wife, Simone. He had retired from teaching and was writing books, lecturing, and hosting a radio show about the English language.

This time, we bought a substantial two-story home in the woods about five miles outside of Columbus. It was a cedar-shingled, green-roofed house that vaguely reminded me of a ski lodge. It had been built in the 1970s, so we made some upgrades. We put in wood floors, updated the kitchen, and added a deck in the rear, overlooking the pines and aspens on the twenty acres surrounding the property. Adding to the ski lodge atmosphere was the fact that we relied heavily on a wood stove for warmth.

It really felt like a world apart, and the ten-minute drive up from Columbus was beautiful. Crossing the Yellowstone and Stillwater rivers, dotted with fly fishermen, past sheep and cattle grazing, you'd drive up a curving road that afforded a brief view of the dramatic Beartooth Mountains and pull off onto a gravel road and down into our dirt driveway.

For all of the problems I'd had dealing with change early in my life, by this point I was able to handle it with relative ease. And this was my new life: most mornings I would strap my kids in the Suburban and then drive into town for breakfast at Uncle Sam's Eatery, a small café with a Yankee Doodle theme housed in a sheet-metal building with a fake log-cabin front. It was situated across the street from a rarely used grain elevator. Then I would take the kids over to play among the cottonwoods at Itch-Kep-Pe Park, a tiny strip of public access along the Yellowstone River.

Then we would come home and I would sit at a small desk in the kitchen playing online poker, earning $40 an hour while nursing my kids. And maybe once a week I would drive to Billings, and then maybe once a month fly down to Las Vegas to play. Or we would all drive down to Las Vegas and stay with Howard so I could play. Depending on who would come down with me, Ben or my mom would take care of the kids, changing diapers, cooking meals, and feeding them bottles while I went to work at the Bellagio, which had eclipsed the Mirage as the place to play high-stakes poker.

One night in September 1999, I was in a really good game, a $300-$600 game in which a player kept "throwing" my bets back. He was a fish who seemed more than willing to continue losing huge pots. I hadn't intended to play late, but I really had to stick around because the game was too profitable to leave.

At around midnight, Ben phoned me on my cell to tell me

he just couldn't handle the kids on his own. They were still up—with no interest in falling asleep. I told him I couldn't just leave, that I was in the middle of a game. He phoned again, maybe an hour later, growing angrier by the second, even though the kids had finally fallen asleep. Again, I told him I couldn't leave. I was winning most of the pots.

It was eleven a.m. when I finally made it back to Howard's, and Ben was beyond pissed that I had been out all night playing poker. But I was living in Montana and commuting to Las Vegas largely because he wanted to live up there, and I had to take advantage of high-stakes poker prospects on the rare occasions that they presented themselves.

He backed off when he learned I'd earned $40,000 for my all-nighter at the Bellagio—enough to pay for a couple of investment properties in Montana. Somehow, it didn't seem fair to be battling for the right to work.

23

Monday, May 10, 2004
9:50 P.M.

WE'RE PLAYING AT $6,000-$12,000 LIMITS. I want to get this over with as quickly as possible. I've been playing in this tournament for two days, which is long enough. I decide to semi-bluff Ron.

I flop a straight draw and a low draw. He bets and I raise.

He folds.

Then there are a couple of hands where I just have the nuts.

We're up to $8,000-$16,000 limits.

I look over and see Howard entering Benny's Bullpen. My brother doesn't ordinarily move quickly, but this time he does. I envision him running up the escalator to make sure he catches the final moments of this tournament. He greets me with a wide smile as he joins my friends. Everyone's cheering. Howard asks me to lean to my left, so he can take in my towers of chips.

It looks like a small city sitting there on the felt. A glorious, colorful city of chips.

By contrast, Ron is getting close to the felt. He has around $28,000 in chips, which isn't much when you have to toss in the blinds, and when your first two bets are $8,000 and the second two are $16,000. With stakes like these, your chips go fast.

I raise on the button to $16,000. He reraises me to $24,000.

Then I raise him back to $28,000.

Looking resigned, he pushes in his remaining $4,000.

We turn over our cards. I have A-2-3-Q, with three spades.

He has 10-8-5-3, with three spades, too.

This is a great hand matchup. The board comes. . . .

K-Q-J-3.

I have queens and threes, which he can't beat!

He's dead in the water.

I feel a jolt of electricity. In the slow-motion version that I remember, I get up and graciously shake Ron's hand with both of my hands, like I'm some kind of diplomat, while he looks at me, a bit dazed. I turn around and hug Howard, and then, propelled by God knows what, I jump on Howard as he stands there. I don't know what I was thinking—he has a bad back! Then I hug my friends two at a time. Then I sit back down at the table where I just won my first World Series of Poker bracelet and start crying as Matt Savage, who had told me early in the tournament that he was "one hundred percent certain" I would win a World Series event, gently places the bracelet on the green felt in front of me.

I cry some more. Can you believe it? I'm actually crying.

Then Howard reaches over and slips the bracelet onto my right wrist, as cameras flash. The ESPN crew, which had been filming Crystal Doan and Millie Shiu bickering in their heads-up battle for the Ladies Tournament, turn their cameras and lights and sound equipment in my direction, as I start to cry again.

As I wipe the tears away with the back of my hand, I say, "I bet you've never seen a boy cry when they've won." Now I'm laughing. "I guess I'm just a girl after all. Just a girl." I pose for the camera.

Just a girl with $137,860.

24

AFTER BEN GOT OVER BEING MAD about my all-night poker game at the Bellagio, we had unbelievable makeup sex, which led to my being pregnant with Lucy.

I was thirty-eight weeks along by the time the 2000 World Series of Poker rolled around. Tired, cranky, hormonal, and fat, I literally could have delivered my third-born amid the thick secondhand smoke of Benny's Bullpen, where the tournaments had moved. I looked about as good as I felt, in my gray maternity shirt and black stretch pants, with swollen bare feet. I weighed 190 pounds.

But that's when I really learned how to bluff more effectively.

I was in a situation where I was the best player at the table. The people around me were inexperienced. They showed all the classic signs. When they were uncomfortable with a hand, their blink rates increased. When they were pleased with their hands, they would look calm. There's no way they could have had a pair of aces without me knowing it. I had tremendous control over the table. People were deferring to me. I would raise. They would fold. I could try out things without much risk. And it really brought my game to another level—realizing that I had a dead read on my opponents.

But then my self-assuredness came back to bite me. By day three I was feeling very pregnant: extremely uncomfortable and not that focused. Until that point, I had actually buckled down and concentrated well for the main event. But at that point, I had been playing for three straight days, and I found myself sitting across the kidney-shaped table from Jim McManus, the future author of *Positively Fifth Street*, whose amateurish—albeit winning—style of play had been the subject of countless discussions among poker's top-ranked professionals. I had never played with the man before.

With a little more than $500,000 in chips, I was enjoying my status as chip leader. There were eighteen players left, total. First place would bring in $1.5 million, so I had a lot on the line. It was the last hand before dinner and I needed the break. I wasn't getting good hands. So with a pair of queens, on the button, I raised.

McManus was in the small blind. He had quite a few chips, but I had more than he did. He reraised, a move that built the pot up to about $100,000.

I knew he was inexperienced. Because I had heard from other people that he had a tendency to overvalue his hands, I moved in, thinking I had the best hand. He called quickly.

It turned out that he had two kings.

I felt awful. I didn't need to gamble $375,000. I went from being chip leader to going to dinner with only $130,000 in chips, which isn't a good sign at the World Series of Poker. I had assumed he had a hand that was underdog to me and I was wrong. Despite all the leaps I had made reading people the day before, the stress of pregnancy had gotten to me—I wasn't reading people well at all. Then he started disparaging me. I was waddling off to dinner when I heard him say, "Why would she move in with queens? It's a real amateur thing to do." He was right, sort of. I didn't need to play with two queens. Ordinarily, I would have called him. But I was just tired. And so unbearably pregnant.

I went to dinner tortured by the play. Then, after we returned to the table, I paid closer attention to his style. Like many men who face me for the first time, he kept calling when he should have folded. I realized that I actually *had* made the right move. After that, I did okay. I got my stack back up to $500,000. I came in tenth place—and became the highest-ranking woman ever at the World Series. I won $52,000.

A month later, Lucy was born. My mom and Katy were on hand for the birth. Katy would later write about how my ability to deal with the pain of natural childbirth said a lot about my personality. As Leo played with his favorite toy of the moment—a wooden gun—and as Ben nervously fried chicken in the kitchen, I lay on my bed upstairs, watching the sci-fi movie *The Matrix*.

When the labor pains arrived, I sat in the blue birthing tub that Renee had set up in the center of the room, and there I stayed, writhing in pain, until I felt certain there was something wrong. Renee moved me to the bed and determined that the baby's head was caught on my cervix. As a futuristic action scene took place on-screen, she released the head in a move that was very quick but also unbearably painful. Lucy was born twenty minutes later.

Afterward, I hung out in our home in Montana, content not to travel much for the first year of her life. And when she was eleven months old, we moved back down to Las Vegas. It was my turn to make the choice of where we lived. This time we bought a nice tract house, measuring more than four thousand square feet, on the preferable West Side, in the Lakes area. It even had a decent-sized backyard. The day we moved in, I found out that I was pregnant again.

We had returned to Vegas in part because the commuting from Montana was too much for me. Now I knew I was expecting my fourth baby, so I tried to make the most of the time I had before delivering—playing in very-high-stakes games. On top of that, I had just had a months-long run of bad cards, from which I was having trouble recovering.

And I was not really looking forward to another delivery. The only glitch with having fast labor is that the contractions are really painful. And because it all happens so quickly, you don't get the chance to build up endorphins, which, in the absence of drugs, make a big difference in your level of discomfort. So when I started having labor with Nelly, and had fully intended to have another home delivery, I kind of surprised myself (and everybody else) when I suddenly said, "I can't do this at home this time. I don't want to feel this."

At the hospital I learned that I was dilated to six centimeters and severely dehydrated, most likely from throwing up. (Once I realized I needed to go to the hospital, I got anxious, and, well, you know what happens then.) My labor had simply stopped because I was so freaked out (yes, your mind can actually halt labor).

They set up the epidural tray. I had my first contraction. They put the epidural in. Two hours and four pushes later, there was Nelly.

My new daughter's the only blue-eyed blonde in the family. Like the others, she's beautiful. I'm amazed at how each of my children is so different from the others. Maud is feisty and brilliant. Leo must be the sweetest young man on the planet. Lucy is my princess; she rivals me as the family clothes hog. Nelly is a sparkle, and supremely affectionate.

♦ ♠ ♥ ♣

So, imagine you're six months postpartum. You're nursing your newborn. You come back from a losing night at poker, tired and depressed. You switch on your computer, and there's a raging diatribe against you, posted in a popular poker chat room by a professional poker player—yes, a competitor—attacking everything about you, from your style of play ("unethical") to your personal hygiene ("poor") to your personality ("obnoxious"). Imagine how you'd feel.

Now imagine that it lasts for a year and a half. How do you respond?

You don't. You can't. You try to understand why he's doing it. He considers his best friend and former backer as a competitor to you and figures the only way to build her up is to tear you down. Or he sees similarities between himself and you, the person he is tormenting. You're both outspoken to a fault and talkative at the poker table to the point that it annoys other players. And that somehow bothers him.

True to form, you don't respond aloud; you keep it inside and become overwhelmingly depressed. Since St. Paul's, you've always been sensitive to people not liking you. You've long been insecure about your looks. You start to wonder if others share his opinions.

It gets harder and harder for you to walk into a poker room. While you *do* wash your clothes daily, you haven't quite recovered from your fourth pregnancy, emotionally or physically. You *are* on a losing streak. You go broke. Not broke-broke, as in can't-afford-to-pay-the-mortgage broke. But poker-broke, as in your-bankroll-won't-be-enough-to-cover-enough-games-to-make-money broke.

You haven't played in the 2002 World Series of Poker because someone associated with Binion's has made hostile comments about your brother, but the display of solidarity only reduces your chances of improving your record—which adds even more fuel to your attacker's flame-fest.

Meanwhile, you're emotionally tilted.

Then you play a pot-limit Omaha game and win $300,000.

You're back.

But within a week, you lose it all.

Howard, too, is going through the same emotional swings and also enduring an extremely bad losing streak. He spends four months losing literally every day. He's at a point where he's borrowing money. He gets very heavily into debt trying to keep his bankroll healthy. *He's* losing. *You're* losing. He was staking you in exchange for 35 percent of your winnings at the time. Then he tells you he can't continue losing so much money. "I can't take this, I can't have both of us losing," he says. "I think it's better for us emotionally if we split."

You can't disagree. But for the first time in your poker career, you're on your own.

As a poker player, you simply can't get caught up in bad luck. This is something Howard taught me early on. Bad things will happen to you in poker, and you serve nobody's interest—except your opponents'—by dwelling on ill fortune. It's a complete waste of mental energy.

I know. It's hard. You can feel really cursed playing poker. This is when people sometimes start playing every hand—or playing their hands poorly—because they allow themselves to be affected by their bad luck.

Remember that poker is a brutal game because the edges are never that big.

So if you're in a situation where you can take a hand that's a 2-to-1 favorite over and over again, you're still going to lose it one out of three times. And you can have a poker session where you lose it ten times in a row. It's not statistically surprising to do that when you're only a 2-to-1 favorite, or a 3-to-2 favorite, or a 3-to-1 favorite. You're talking about relatively small edges here. So when you lose several times in a row, it's very important not to allow yourself to let that affect your game.

I was never much of a tilter, but early in my career I definitely would let it get me down, and I would sit at the table and complain about my bad luck. It was one of my biggest faults (along with being a lousy winner and a lousy loser). No doubt my endless complaining was annoying to other players at the table. But it also gave them an edge. If you sit there and moan about your bad luck, you're eroding your table image. People are going to come after you then because they know that you're in a bad mood and you're thinking like a loser.

It's definitely hard to get over that part, especially for someone who is as competitive as I am. It's difficult to develop the mental stamina needed to keep yourself from moaning about your bad luck. Moaning and playing every hand.

My tormentor eventually apologized, in fall 2003, in conjunction with what sounded like a religious awakening he had. He e-mailed me to say that he was sorry for making his malicious attacks on me. Another reason he apologized was that Matt Savage had a conversation in which he told the guy his future in the World Series of Poker was at risk unless he stopped his attacks.

So, he apologized, personally but not publicly, and I wasn't convinced that it was sincere. Turns out I was right. He started up again. Then he backed off. But I never quite know if or when the whole ordeal will rear its ugly head again.

Sometimes it takes getting knocked around a bit to find out who you really are. This online situation made me really examine why I was playing poker in the first place. Nobody probably noticed but me, but at that point, it was very painful for me to walk into a poker room—or even a supermarket—and wonder what people were thinking. It was hard for me to face my peers when I didn't know whether they agreed with him and thought that I was scuzzy and that my clothes stank and that I was a bitch.

The situation forced me to question why I was playing poker to begin with. And I had to be honest with myself. I came to realize that I was playing poker in part because I wanted people to look at me and think that I was great because I was competing in the world's biggest games. Yes, I wanted to be a star. And you know what? That was a stupid reason to be playing. Where was it getting me? I had won $300,000 and lost it in a single week. I wasn't proving anything to anyone, particularly myself.

Poker players at all levels grapple with the same issue I was facing: how do you know when to move up to a higher game? Say you've played $6-$12 with a somewhat successful record, but you're not winning enough money. You think it might be time to move up to $10-$20.

For starters, if you ever see a game that looks really soft at another level, there's absolutely nothing wrong with taking a shot at it. If you don't do well, you could always move back down. Nothing ventured. . . .

But the great moving-up decision should be governed by something else: your bankroll requirement. Let's start at the top. To keep your life on an even keel, you should have a poker bankroll that's separate from your grocery money. That's the first consideration. You don't play until you've secured money for your household needs.

Once you don't have to worry about paying the rent and

other financial concerns, you create a poker bankroll. And the amount of money you put in that bankroll depends on how good you are in the game relative to the risk of ruin. Essentially, you want to have a bankroll that can withstand the variance. So the better you are, the lower the variance that you're going to experience in that game, and the smaller your bankroll can be. The better you are at poker, the less your risk of ruin.

In a limit poker game, you ideally want to have a minimum of three hundred big bets in your bankroll. If you're way better than the typical opponents of the game level you play, you can have fewer big bets in your bankroll—although that would be rare.

I'll do the math for you. If you're going to play \$10-\$20, for example, you want to have somewhere between \$6,000 and \$10,000. That's your poker money. Total. For one game you

Sometimes, the best strategy is to just go home.

Try to never lose an amount that you couldn't win on a very good night. It's rare that you're going to win more than thirty big bets in a game. Once you get past thirty big bets, it becomes very difficult, statistically. When you're losing too much, accept the fact it just isn't your night. Or that you're not playing well. Or that the game's not good. Or that you're getting unlucky. Whatever. Give up and come back the following day. That way, you're never taking that large of a chunk out of your bankroll.

want to be playing with around $600. And you don't want to lose much more than that for two reasons.

First, if you're losing a lot of money in the game you're invariably not playing as well as you could. And, hand in hand with that, you're not going to be the best judge of whether you're playing well. Because you're losing, you're probably going to be psychologically playing from behind.

And if you lose too much, the next day when you come in you'll still be psychologically playing from behind.

In terms of bankroll accumulation, you don't want to move up from a $10-$20 game to a $20-$40 game until you're more toward the $10,000 end of your $6,000–$10,000 bankroll. It's a bigger game. The competition is stiffer. Obviously the risk of ruin is greater.

Again, there's nothing wrong with taking shots at bigger games without a sufficient bankroll, as long as you understand you're taking a shot and that if you lose you have to step back down immediately.

What you don't want to do is the following. Say you play $20-$40 and you lose $1,200. You don't want to say, "Oh, I lost $1,200 playing $20-$40! I'll never win that back playing $10-$20, so I'm going to keep playing $20-$40."

If you're taking a shot, you have to truly take it as a shot. The fact is, if you only have $6,000, you *shouldn't* be playing $20-$40. That's too low of a bankroll, so if you're going to take a shot with a $6,000 bankroll, it better be a really good game, and you should acknowledge that you're just taking a shot, and that if you lose you'll step back down to $10-$20. It doesn't have to be forever.

Likewise, you can move up any time you think a game looks good. But that doesn't necessarily mean you're making a permanent move. What it does mean is that if you do well, you've just added a healthy chunk to your bankroll and maybe you can continue to play $20-$40, assuming the games are good. Or you can alternate between $10-$20 and $20-$40—wherever you find good games.

Sometimes the higher earn is actually in the lower game. If you take a $10-$20 game where there are a lot of bad players, versus a $20-$40 game where there are decent players and only one bad player, I can guarantee that your earn per hour will be more in the $10-$20 game—and it's lower risk.

I needed to figure out what role poker should play in my life, and how I could best approach the game in the interest of keeping it profitable while also maintaining my sanity. I decided to step back for a couple of months and gain some perspective.

Then I had an epiphany—it actually happened while I was folding laundry. I realized that I didn't want to hide from poker for the significant reason that it was what I wanted to do with my life. But I also realized that it didn't make sense to be playing poker for the reasons I had been playing—basically, because I wanted people to look at me a certain way. And because I was trying to prove that I was as good at it as any man.

No, I had to play poker because I wanted to, regardless of what others thought. I love the game. I'm good at it. And it's paying my bills. It bought us a beautiful house. It has helped me build a comfortable life for my family. What I needed to do was sit down and play poker as if I were doing it for myself alone, and not as if I were a performing monkey for people to point at and say, "Look at how high of a game she's playing!" And, inevitably: "For a girl!"

I discovered I wasn't happy playing $1,000-$2,000 in the first place. It's too much financial pressure to play that high, and I didn't need the money that badly. I decided that my self-esteem should not be based on the need to be seen in the highest game in the room. Not only was it misguided as a personal motivation, it also was downright erroneous from a financial perspective. You're playing against the best players in the world, and if you step it down to the $400-$800 level, all of those great players are weeded out of the game and your earn is almost as much anyway. It's much lower variance and it's much lower bankroll stress, and you're not playing against the Doyle Brunsons and the Chip Reeses and the Gus Hansens and the Barry Greensteins.

I've made much more money since I decided to step it back a notch and take my ego out of the equation. But it did take me a year to recover my bankroll. In that time I also realized that I was much happier playing in tournaments than in cash games. And that's when my friend Erik made me a deal I couldn't refuse. He offered to back me in tournaments for a percent of my winnings. I felt relieved of the financial burden of fronting tournament fees, grateful to have such a generous friend, optimistic that everything would work out.

It's an important lesson for any player, but it was crucial for me. If you're doing something to keep up with the Joneses, you're not going to be happy. And you're not going to perform at your peak level. But if you're doing something because it's your passion, and you're doing it at the level at which you're comfortable, you'll do well.

So in a way, I have my online tormentor to thank. His attacks turned out to be a gift to my life. I'm more focused now, and a better player. I'm happier, too.

25

MY VICTORY WAS A CLOUD that I rode throughout the glorious night of May 10, 2004, and into the magnificent morning of May 11. After descending the escalator from Benny's Bullpen, I joyfully dialed up a succession of friends on my cell phone as we headed en masse to the Bellagio to celebrate. "I won!" I kept repeating to people on the other end. At some point, I started losing track of who it was that I had phoned. Had I called my agent? My mom? My dad? Renee? "I won!" I shrieked as I ordered bottles of Belvedere in Caramel, the sleek, dark bar near the entrance to the Bellagio's poker room. They brought the bottles on a cart bearing ice, lime, tonics, cranberry juice, and other mixers. I sat on an oversized leather stool as friends surrounded me, toasting my victory. I brought with me the cash, which I would later stuff into a friend's safe-deposit box in the Bellagio, because there was too much of it to fit into my own box, which would only hold about $100,000.

I phoned my kids. It was shortly after ten and Maud was still up and excited to hear about my win.

We hung out in Caramel for hours. Actually, we sort of took over the bar. The party had expanded in size and then—I have no idea how long we were there—we moved as a boisterous, happy jumble through the forest of slot machines and over to Light, the Bellagio's nightclub. A manager greeted me with a congratulatory hug—how does everybody in Las Vegas always know what's going on at any given moment?—and we were all escorted past hundreds of would-be partiers who were waiting to gain entrance, and into the far reaches of the club, where a group of cozy tables had been reserved for VIPs.

That would be us.

There was more Belvedere, and more celebratory hugs, and there was dancing. To music that kept me floating on my cloud for hours, bringing me back, temporarily, to the euphoria of my New York club nights. At one point I turned to the random person beside me on the dance floor and said, "I won! Can you believe it? I won!"

By five—or was it six?—dawn had cast a rosy glow over the Las Vegas valley, and a friend drove me back to Howard's house. The sun poured in like honey on Mt. Charleston in the west. I tiptoed into the spare bedroom, where Lucy and Nelly were sleeping on opposite sides of the bed, looking safe and happy. Cautiously, I slipped in between my two little women, careful not to disturb their slumber. Then I quietly pulled the blanket over my shoulders, settling in.

I belonged.

26

I HAD FOUR GREAT KIDS. My poker career was back on track. And I was able to leverage my success in areas that promised to take the pressure off of my game. A book deal. A pending movie deal. A pending sitcom deal. But go to the Internet chat rooms where professional players and fans air their thoughts and you quickly detect a division in the poker community. Some purists are convinced that certain professionals like me have become shameless self-promoters, with our publicists, agents, managers, and anyone else out there to extend our "brand."

But think about it. Poker's rise in popularity has allowed us to become less dependent on a game that can—on the turn of a card or on a lapse in self-discipline—quickly grind professionals into grit. So when opportunity knocks—when I have the option to hedge my bets by generating non-poker income—I race to answer the door.

Go ahead. Call me a media whore. I can take it.

And while I tend to be suspicious of people who start statements with, "And it's not all about the money," the fact is, it's *not* all about the money. I enjoy new intellectual challenges. So when a software company called ieLogic, Inc., which develops multiplayer poker software for the Internet, approached me in 2000 to start discussing the possibility of representing their proposed poker Web site as a celebrity player, I didn't even pretend to play hard to get.

Along with my friend Phil Hellmuth, I became associated with the new site that would use excapsa software: ultimatebet.com. The deal was that when the site finally went live a year later, I would play on it and be compensated for being one of the celebrity players.

But when the site did go live, I kept calling the company with suggestions about how the software should be altered, recommending new capabilities to be introduced. It got to the point where they offered to hire me as a consultant. I couldn't refuse.

Yes, I was displaying the same workaholic tendencies that my father showed so many years earlier. (And still shows, by the way. I've lost track of how many books he has published on topics ranging from naughty puns to palindromes to punctuation, and I'm always running across articles he has written and hearing him on his radio talk show.) But I was feeling the need to branch out into as many moneymaking ventures as possible. As my poker career and its ancillary enterprises became more stable, my marriage started to crumble. I felt tremendous financial pressure—and that meant taking advantage of every opportunity that came my way, and some that I would have to chase down. I was concerned about my family's future.

Actually, I needed to do a number of things, including get out of Las Vegas. Las Vegas is a phenomenal place if you're a cosmetic surgeon—the city is a fertile market of women who'll pay big time for better boobs—but it isn't particularly good for children. Forget the transience, forget the superficiality, forget the emphasis on the ludicrous and the lascivious. (I'm no prude, but I really couldn't warm up to a lifestyle of driving my kids around to their activities and hearing radio commercials touting "ten-dollar lap dances for locals" or having my children point to the numerous billboards depicting naked women.) The climate alone is enough to discourage anyone from raising kids there: how can you expect children to enjoy their summers off from school when they can't even leave the house because it's 120 degrees in the shade and the mere act of playing on the monkey bars is likely to leave them with second-degree burns?

By the spring of 2003 I had been devoting an inordinate amount of time to consulting with ieLogic, and they finally asked me if I would consider moving close to their headquarters at the time in Portland, Oregon. It was a great break, and I was eager to check it out.

After the two-hour flight, I stepped off the plane and drove through greenery and lovely established neighborhoods with shaded, two-story bungalows with wide porches and solid Tudors with inviting front lawns. There were parks and preschools and bicyclists and the sound of lawn edgers. By the time I reached the company's offices, I had already decided that this was where I wanted to raise my kids. I could fly down to Las Vegas whenever I needed to play in tournaments. While there, I could hang out with friends. But Portland would be our family home.

So, in July 2003, we moved. We bought a thick-walled Craftsman bungalow up on a little knoll and filled it with shabby-chic furniture and wildlife artwork and earth tones and classical literature—it wasn't quite what you'd expect for a professional gambler's home. It seemed more suitable for, say, a bank vice president in the 1920s. We had oak floors and a porch swing and a huge picture window overlooking the front-yard rhododendron. And we loved it.

We positioned a play structure with swings in the backyard. The kids called it "Rainbow trout." (It was a Rainbow brand play structure, and they had once gone fishing for rainbow trout with their father—hence the name.) We were raising a family in an environment that seemed more perfect than anything I could have envisioned.

But even this wholesome setting couldn't disguise the obvious: Ben and I could not stay married. He was a different person than I thought he was, which wasn't surprising because we had never dated. And I had gotten married for some of the wrong reasons—basically to escape my life, and because as an ambitious person I had thought I wanted to spend the rest of my life with someone who was less ambitious.

I'm also somebody who would be very difficult to be married to. Not necessarily because I don't take the traditional woman's role, but because I can be very stubborn. I don't like anyone to get in my way. I can be argumentative, and I'm not the easiest person on the planet to argue with. I don't like to be wrong. That's tough on a marriage. And I'm not necessarily a great compromiser in a relationship.

But neither of us was.

One thing that makes poker so appealing is that you can fold your cards if your hand doesn't look promising. In any other game that the house offers you, you don't have a choice but to play. You stick your quarter in the slot machine or the video poker machine that deals you a hand—and you still have to play it. (Okay, okay—Caribbean Stud gives you a fold option.) But in blackjack, in baccarat, in virtually every other game you're forced to play the hand. In poker, much of your edge comes from the fact that you can choose which hands you play and which hands you don't. That gives you amazing control.

It was time to take control of our lives. So in November 2003, Ben and I separated and laid plans for a divorce. And I found something far more painful than losing at a final table to the only card in a deck that can beat you—trying not to break down into tears when your four-year-old asks for maybe the seventeenth time: "When's Daddy coming home?"

27

My win in the Omaha Hi-Lo Split accomplished much more than merely securing my position at the top of the heap among female poker players. It established my credibility as one of the best poker players, irrespective of gender. Imagine: if I had played in the Ladies event and managed to win it, I would still hear that I was being touted as such a hotshot poker player *for a woman*.

Not only did the event mark a turning point from a now-we-don't-need-to-use-the-W-word perspective, but it also attracted the attention of folks who somehow must have assumed that because I hadn't won a World Series event, I couldn't truly be considered among poker's elite.

So in August 2004, it came to pass that ESPN and Harrah's Entertainment wanted to gather ten top poker players, shut them in a conference room in the Rio All-Suites Hotel and Casino for hours of No-Limit Texas Hold 'em, and give the ultimate winner $2 million. It would make poker history if only for one major detail: the Tournament of Champions, as they chose to call it, would become the first time that a network—as opposed to players—offered to put up the prize pool.

Harrah's polled the players in the 2004 World Series to identify the best No-Limit Texas Hold 'em players in the world, and I was among those named. Then the sponsors had to narrow it down to ten participants, and I was selected. Was it because they needed a woman? Was it because I had a relatively strong camera presence? These theories, and many more, circulated on the Internet in the weeks prior to the event, which took place on September 2, 2004.

After my learning experience with my online tormentor, I was smart enough not to spend too much time reading what people were writing about me, or pondering the rationale. I was just happy to be included, along with nine others. They were, in alphabetical order:

Doyle Brunson—the elder statesman at the table, looking natty in his white Stetson and dark sport jacket.

Johnny Chan—with his trademark orange placed on the table in front of him.

T. J. Cloutier—square-jawed and gray-haired, wearing a well-pressed black shirt.

Phil Hellmuth—wearing a black Oakley cap and a black Oakley sweatshirt.

Phil Ivey—looking wide-eyed in a white, red, and black workout suit.

Howard Lederer—a dominating table presence with classic good looks, wearing a blue cotton T-shirt.

Daniel Negreanu—with his multiple earrings, tinted blond hair tips, and wearing a long-sleeve light-blue shirt.

Greg Raymer—baby-faced, wearing funky green shades and a shirt decorated with fish.

Chip Reese—the cash-game king wears a blue shirt, too. It matches his blue eyes. He must have been perfect blue-eyed, blond-haired teen idol material.

It was a welcome endorsement. I had done relatively poorly in the World Series of Poker's final event, with its record 2,576 participants, bluffing my money off with king high to place 248th. *Yes, you lose some.* Now I had a chance to shine.

The rules of this tournament were unusual. Nobody other than the ten players and the relevant ESPN and Harrah's employees were to know the identity of the winner until the shoot-out's initial airdate of September 21. As we gathered for this first-of-its-kind tournament, we signed agreements indicating that the act of leaking the winner's name could cost us $5 million. I didn't mind signing the deal; I can keep a secret.

There was something symbolic about this moment in poker history, best articulated by Rob Gillespie, president of Bodog.com Sportsbook and Casino. "When an organization as reputable as ESPN launches their own tournament, you know that this is no longer just a fad. It is becoming a mainstream interest," he said. His words were quoted in a press release that listed the participants' odds to win.

Daniel Negreanu, who had been named Toyota Player of

the Year at the 2004 World Series of Poker, was ranked as the early odds-on favorite to win. He was listed at 4-to-1 odds.

Phil Ivey had 5-to-1 odds.

I was tied with T. J. Cloutier and Phil Hellmuth with 10-to-1 odds—not quite as bad as the long-shot player, 2004 World Series of Poker Champion Greg Raymer, whose odds were 15 to 1.

When we finally sat down at that table, each of us had $200,000 in starting chips. I eyed my opponents, and it immediately struck me that we all had one thing in common: nobody in this group was likely to make big mistakes. Daunted, I set a goal for myself: I just didn't want to be the first player knocked out.

I thought I might not reach that goal during an early hand against Daniel. He raised on the button and I reraised out of the small blind, holding a pair of 10s.

The board came K-7-5 (two hearts).

I bet. He called. As he did, he said something that made me think he just might have hit his hand.

On the turn, I checked and he checked.

On the river I checked. He bet.

So I folded. Later, when I watched the broadcast, I saw that he had A-K, so Daniel had definitely hit his hand. But the early loss got me down to about $160,000 in chips.

That hand made me the short stack until Phil Hellmuth and Chip Reese ended up in a hand together. Chip was crippled when his pair of kings couldn't hold up against Phil's aces. Shortly afterward, Chip was knocked out.

I felt relieved: at least I wasn't the first to go.

Soon, T. J. got knocked out, too.

That's when I realized I needed a special strategy for this

tournament. Until that point, I had been playing small-pot poker. That wouldn't work with this crowd. I needed to catch a break and build up my stack and then devise a strategy better suited to a tournament, where it didn't matter if I moved up a notch—I had to win it *all*.

I'm accustomed to being the most aggressive player at any table, which was probably true of everyone in the Tournament of Champions, and I had to take into account that any one of my opponents could match my ability to bluff, trap, or, in general, outplay. I had to figure out a way to feel in control, to reverse my feelings of being somewhat overwhelmed by the level of competition. I bolstered my chip position to $130,000 when my pair of kings held up against Daniel's 7-5 (hearts). Comforted for the moment, I was able to focus on revising my strategy.

Then I started noticing something about my brother's play. As the blinds and antes increased, Howard began moving in a lot. By putting in his chips before the flop, he was essentially taking away his opponents' opportunities to make decisions later in the hand. It was a way for Howard to deny his opponents the chance to outthink him later.

Ordinarily, great players don't want to get all their money in before the flop—they want to be able to make as many decisions as they can, in order to outthink and outplay their opponents multiple times throughout a hand. Denying them those decisions increases variance and is akin to forcing them to gamble.

It made perfect sense. In a winner-take-all tournament like this, against players who don't *make* bad decisions, the act of taking away opponents' opportunities to decide can become a powerful weapon.

That's the strategy I chose to deploy. Since it was Howard's strategy, too, it would be more painful if I were to butt up against him because a lot of chips would be at stake. But strategy or not, I still needed good cards. It happened quickly. Phil Ivey moved in. With A-Q (spades), I moved in behind him, having him slightly covered. Howard moved in behind me. He had a monster chip stack and had me well covered. I suspected he had a very good hand. In fact, he turned over K-K. Ivey turned over A-8. The board gave us two spades, and there was a spade on the turn. I made my flush, tripling up in chips to about $290,000. I also knocked Ivey out of the tournament.

I barely had time to breathe a sigh of relief when I landed an incredibly interesting hand. Daniel opened the pot in first position for about $36,000. I had a pair of 10s. I felt Daniel was weak, so I reraised him all-in—he had another $90,000 in chips. Everyone folded around to Greg in the big blind. Greg had amassed a dominating stack by playing a controlled game. He had about $450,000 to start the hand. He moved in. Daniel quickly folded.

That left me in a precarious position. There was $450,000 in the pot. I had $150,000 left. I would get 3-to-1 odds to call my last $150,000. Those are huge odds.

So I had to try to determine what Greg was holding.

If Greg had A-K, I'd be the 6-to-5 favorite. That's an easy call when the pot odds are 3 to 1. But if he had an overpair, I would be at a 4-to-1 disadvantage—an easy fold with 3-to-1 pot odds. If both A-K and an overpair are possibilities, it would be mathematically correct to call.

I considered the hand more closely. Greg knew that Daniel

had raised out of first position—a sign of a strong hand. Greg knew that I had reraised Daniel out of second position, making it highly unlikely that I was bluffing. Because I had left myself only $150,000 in chips, he also must have seen me as being pot-committed, with the possibility of getting 3 to 1 on the pot. As such, he probably figured it was unlikely that I would fold.

Greg also knew that I knew that he knew this.

Meanwhile, I observed a tell on Greg that indicated he was comfortable with his hand.

So I thought about Greg's style of play. Given all he knew about my hand, would he really risk all his chips with A-K? Answer: no. I figured the same could be said for J-J and Q-Q. I decided he probably had A-A or K-K. So I folded.

Throughout the dinner break that followed, I was haunted by the fact that I had tripled up and then, in a single hand, been knocked down to $150,000. To compound matters, my good pal Phil Hellmuth tried to convince me that I shouldn't have folded; he was certain that Greg had A-K.

Right after dinner, Doyle knocked Daniel out. Then Howard knocked out Doyle.

We were down to five.

Still short-stacked and facing increasing blinds, I was dealt A-4 (hearts). I figured it might be the best hand I would have during this round of play. Greg raised on the button. He could have anything, I thought, because good players will raise a large range of hands on the button. I moved in. For Greg, who was getting 2 to 1 from the pot, it would be an automatic call with any two cards. He called with 9-8 (clubs). It was no match for my ace high, and I doubled up in chips.

I doubled through him again on a subsequent hand, even though he was playing very well. And then I knocked him out with a pair of 8s. As we shook hands, he whispered in my ear, "I had kings on that hand." What an awesome guy he was to put my mind at ease.

And to give me an extra shot of confidence.

I was chip leader, with $680,000 in chips. But the fact is, I felt as if I faced a death squad when I looked at my remaining opponents around the table. Howard. Phil Hellmuth. Johnny Chan. I felt intimidated—but prepared.

Wielding a pair of 6s, Johnny won a big hand against my brother, who held A-J. Ironically, Phil would have won that hand if he hadn't folded his A-Q, leaving my brother to tell Phil, "My only satisfaction in losing that hand is that you would have won it." Funny.

The joke turned out to be on Johnny, who took a very bad beat against Phil losing with kings to Phil's tens. Crippled, Johnny was forced to go all-in with Q-J and was out of the tournament.

So there we were: my good friend Phil; my brother-mentor, Howard; and me. I sat at one end of the table; they occupied the other. Phil was chip leader. I was second. Howard was third. I considered Howard to be the best player at the table and preferred to go heads-up with Phil instead.

I got my chance.

At that point, the antes were $4,000 and the blinds were $12,000-$24,000.

I was on the button holding a pair of 6s. I opened with $72,000. Phil folded. My brother, who was playing very aggressively, moved in. Because he had been moving in on lots of hands, I didn't take it to mean much. Those 6s were supposed to be the best hand, and I also had Howard covered—so I couldn't go broke making the easy call.

Resting his chin in his hand, Howard turned over a pair of 7s.

"Nice hand, Bub," I said. The tables had turned. Now I was more than a 4-to-1 underdog.

This would be painful, I thought. Losing so many chips. If he won, I would be giving him nearly half of my stack.

The room was silent.

Then came the board: 6-Q-Q. Amazingly, I had flopped a set of 6s! I was at once elated and devastated. I was ecstatic that I now stood to go heads-up in the biggest game of my life. And, as chip leader, I actually had a good chance to win. But . . . that meant my brother could go out on a bad beat.

The turn was a 9. (No help for Howard.) The river: a 3. Howard lost to my full house.

It was like a kick to my stomach. I couldn't hold back my tears as I rose from my chair and hugged Howard, telling him I was sorry. Then I couldn't stop weeping. Viewers of the Tournament of Champions never knew this, but we had to take a break as I left the room, crying. I didn't even stop to put on my shoes.

I returned to play heads-up with Phil Hellmuth. Both of us were wearing black, and it kind of fit the mood. We both sat on the same side of the table, but at opposite ends. They dumped the $2 million in cash onto the green felt between us. I tried not to let it distract me. But, come on. . . .

Like me, Phil tends to be a bit misunderstood. He's a better player than I am, but if you catch him at the right time, he can get unhinged. Part of Phil's strategy involves trying to get players mad at him at the table. He'll insult your ability to play. Most folks fall for this tactic and get defensive, which hurts their game. They try to go after him and, lost in their aggression, they lose a lot of money to him.

But I try to outfox him. I just laugh and agree with him when he implies that I'm not playing well. "I never said I was good, I'm just trying to get lucky," I say. Or, "You're right. I'm not a good player and I'm really lucky to be heads-up with you."

It's a total dead end for such people because they don't know what to do. It takes all the wind out of their sails. It takes all the power they have away from them. It's like the reflective shield that shines the laser beam right back at them.

The psychology I opted to use against Phil was to agree with him and just get him off kilter. And it worked.

By that time we had played in this tournament for nearly twelve tense hours. Heads-up, we traded the chip lead back and forth. At one point, he doubled through me, putting me at a 2-to-1 chip disadvantage, when we both had a trip of 3s but he had a better kicker. But I kept my cool.

I bluffed four hands in a row and then decided to put my feet on the brakes. He kept saying over and over to me: "You're reckless." At the point that I decided I was done bluffing, I kept saying, "Why aren't you calling me? You know I've been bluffing you. If you think I'm overcommitting my chips you should be calling me. If you're smart enough to figure out that I'm bluffing, why aren't you calling?"

My voice was quiet and strained from fatigue. I was basically daring him, saying, "Go with your read. If you think I'm bluffing, you should call me." And it got him to call me.

So, heading into the final hand, I had $1,460,000 in chips to Phil's $540,000.

Phil limped in on the button.

I checked in the big blind with K-10.

The flop came 2-10-7. I checked.

He bet $45,000.

I raised to $200,000, putting the pressure on him.

Phil went all-in with $450,000.

There was $830,000 in the pot.

I called.

Phil turned over his 10-8 (unsuited). We each had a pair. My king was the better kicker.

We both stood up. I covered my mouth with my hands; it's the sort of involuntary gesture you might make if you just heard about a devastating natural disaster or were just named Miss America.

Voice-over: *"Annie's overcome with emotion, seeing how close she is to winning this championship. . . ."*

The turn: a 7. No help for Phil.

"Annie Duke is now one card away from two million dollars. . . ."

He needed an 8 to win.

We stared at the table, anticipating the river card. It was a . . .

3!

"Annie Duke has defeated nine of the strongest poker players in the world and wins the first-ever World Series of Poker Tournament of Champions."

It took a couple of seconds for the reality to sink in. I had just won $2 million!

I gave Phil a hug. It was all happening in slow motion.

I hugged the dealer.

"Oh my God! I won!" I yelled.

I wiped away tears and then said, "All right, let me call my brother." Then I found myself saying, "Oh my God, Howard, I'm sorry about the sixes. . . ."

Phil was in heavy reaction mode, spouting off to no one in particular: "She check-raised me six times. I know she didn't have it six times." That was the first sentence of a rambling rant-athon that was captured on film.

When people ask me whether I felt insulted by Phil's now-famous, televised Philalogue, I produce a simple answer: "How could I be insulted? I'm the one with the trophy, right?"

At 3:30 a.m., in the heart of Las Vegas, Howard Greenbaum, Harrah's Vice President of Specialty Gambling, presented me with my trophy and my $2 million in cash. I broke into a silly grin. Not bad for twelve hours of work, I thought, as I posed before the video camera. Or twelve hours that was three decades in the making.

Soon I was thinking about everything that this exasperating and thrilling card game has given me. Poker has helped me gain an invaluable perspective on my life. It has really helped me understand emotional control and patience. Even better, it's helped me accept that there's nothing that can happen to you that's so bad that you can't handle it. You have bad things happen to you constantly when you're playing poker, and you just end up realizing that, in the end, how bad can it be?

Oh, yes. And the two-mil-*yun* dol-*lahs.* There's that, too.

But maybe that's just the bonus.

Words to Play By

Poker has its own lexicon. Here's a list of some of the more common poker terms. It proves helpful when I describe my World Series of Poker play.

ace-high A five-card hand with an ace but no pair. It loses to any pair or higher hand but beats a king-high.

aces-up A pair of aces with any other pair.

action The bets and raises.

aggressive Style of play of those who raise and reraise, often to scare people out of pots.

all-in When you bet all your remaining chips.

ante The opening bet before dealing begins.

back door Making your hand with the last two cards. She made a "back-door flush."

bad beat Losing a hand that you were favored to win, as when there are only four cards in the deck that can beat you and your opponent catches one of those cards. The term also implies that the winner had no business being in the pot because he or she was playing against the odds.

belly buster An inside straight draw.

bet the pot Betting the total value of the money in the pot.

bicycle The lowest possible hand in Omaha, A-2-3-4-5 (a.k.a. a wheel).

big bets In limit games, the third bet (after the turn) and fourth bet (after the river) are double the amount of the first bet (before the flop) and second bet (after the flop).

blank A card that has no value for all hands.

blind The forced bet made by the two players to the left of the dealer (or button). The first player bets the "small blind" (say, $5), and the second player must bet double that ($10) for the "big blind."

bluff Betting with a weak hand with the intention of getting your opponent to fold.

board The faceup community cards in Texas Hold 'em or Omaha.

boat Slang for a full house.

bottom pair A pair made with the lowest card on the flop.

broadway The term for an ace-high straight.

bullets Slang for a pair of aces in the hole.

bump To raise a bet.

buried A pair in the first two hole cards. ("He had buried tens.")

burn The dealer "burns" a card—discards a card from the top of the deck—before dealing the flop, turn, and river.

bust a player To eliminate a player from a tournament.

busted hand A hand that has less value than a pair. ("She had a busted flush.")

button The little disk placed in front of the person who would be dealing if everyone had a chance to deal. It rotates clockwise around the table. The player "on the button" is the last to receive cards on the deal and the last to bet.

buy-in The amount in chips required to play in a tournament, as in "the Limit Hold 'em tournament had a $1,500 buy-in."

buying the pot Making a bet so large that other players are unlikely to call.

call To match the current bet.

calling down To just call on the river with a weak hand.

calling station A player who routinely calls and is therefore hard to bluff.

cap The limit on the amount of raises in a betting round.

catching cards Getting favorable cards.

chase You're chasing when you stay in against a stronger hand, hoping to outdraw it.

check To defer making the first bet in a round until someone else has bet.

check-raise To first check and then raise a bet in a betting round. This is typically done to limit the field if you are in early position, or to trap someone to bet in order to make the pot bigger if you have a very strong hand and think someone behind you will bet. (Also called sandbagging.)

cold call To call a raise when you haven't yet bet.

connectors Cards of consecutive ranks. If they're of the same suit, you refer to them as "suited connectors."

counterfeit To make your hand less valuable by a board card that duplicates a card in your hand.

cowboys Slang for kings.

dead hands Hands that have no chance of winning the pot.

deuce Slang for two.

dog Short for underdog.

donkey A bad player. This is a term that's best used in the first person—nobody wants to call any other player a donkey. It is permissible, though, to trash others' play by citing specifics, as in: "I don't know why she would play jack-queen after he raised her on the turn." The word can also be used as a verb, as in, "I *donked* off all my money before the break."

down cards Hole cards.

down to the felt Out of chips.

draw Sometimes in poker you have a made hand and sometimes you have a draw hand. An example of a made hand is when you have two pair. A draw hand is when you have nothing at the moment—like four hearts but no pair. You're trying to complete the hand by drawing a fifth heart. That's a flush draw.

drawing dead A drawing hand that will lose even if it improves.

draw out To catch a card that turns your hand from a losing hand to a winning hand.

edge Mathematical advantage.

expected value The average amount of money a hand will make or lose.

face cards Jacks, queens, and kings.

favorite The hand most likely to win.

fish A bad player. (Also called a whale.)

flat call The act of calling without raising.

flop The first three faceup community cards in Texas Hold 'em or Omaha. Also means catching a card on the flop, as in, "I flopped a set."

flush Five cards of the same suit.

fold When you decline to bet and therefore relinquish your chances of competing for the pot.

four flush When your hole cards, combined with the board, make four cards to a flush. You need to hit only one more card of that suit for a flush.

free card When everyone checks and you get to see the turn or river card without having to call a bet.

free rolling When you have locked up the high or low to share the pot in Omaha while still having a chance of winning it all.

grinder Someone who plays in a style that only wins her a little bit of money each session.

gut-shot straight draw When you need one specific rank card to make a straight. Say you've got 6-7. The flop comes 4-9-10. Only one card—an 8—will make your straight. You've got four outs.

heads-up A game between two players, as in the last two players in a tournament. Also referred to as head-to-head.

hit To obtain a card you need.

implied odds Adjusting the pot odds to account for future betting.

inside straight Four cards that require one in the middle for a straight. (Also known as a belly buster.)

isolate You isolate a player by raising, with the intention of removing everyone else from the hand except for that player.

kicker The highest unpaired card in your hand that is not part of a flush or straight.

ladies A pair of queens.

limp in To open the pot with a call, sometimes with the intention of raising later.

lock A hand that is guaranteed to win at least half of the pot.

loose Playing too liberally for the odds. A loose player might play A-J in early position.

middle pair If the flop has cards of three different ranks and you make a pair with the middle-ranked card, you have a middle pair.

move in To bet all of your chips.

muck The pile of facedown discarded cards. Also used to refer to the act of folding one's hand (and tossing into the muck), as in, "I mucked my hand."

no-limit Any version of poker in which a player may bet any amount of chips (up to the number in front of him) when it's his turn to bet.

nut flush The highest possible flush. It's usually an ace-high flush, but it could also be a straight flush.

nuts The highest possible hand on a given board. If the board comes 6-4-4-J-Q, the nuts would be four 4s.

nut straight The highest possible straight given what's on the board. If the board comes 5-6-9-K-A, the "nut straight" would be 9 high, requiring hole cards of 7-8.

offsuit Cards not of the same suit.

open Making the first bet.

open-ended straight draw When you can make a straight with either of two rank cards. Say you have 9-10 and the flop comes 5-J-Q. You can make a straight with either a king or an 8. You have eight outs.

outs Remaining cards that could improve your hand.

overcard A card in your hand that is higher than those on the board. Say the flop comes 7-10-J. The ace and queen in your hand are overcards.

overpair A pocket pair that is higher than the highest card on the board.

passive Style of play of those who tend to call and rarely raise.

play back at To reraise.

play the board To play a hand that doesn't require any of your hole cards, but instead includes all five board cards. With such a hand, the best you can do is split the pot.

pocket cards Hole cards.

pot limit A game in which the largest bet possible is equal to the total amount of money in the pot.

pot odds The ratio determined by calculating the amount of money in the pot versus the cost of a bet or a call. If the pot contains $40, and it costs $10 to call, the pot odds are $40 to $10, or 4 to 1. In poker lingo, the pot is laying you 4-to-1 odds.

protect Betting in the hope of getting others to fold.

put down To fold.

quads Four of a kind.

railbird Spectator.

raise The act of calling and increasing the previous bet.

rags Useless cards.

Razz A form of Seven-Card Stud in which low hands win.

rebuy To pay an additional entry fee to continue playing in a tournament.

reraise Raising a raiser.

river The fifth and final community card in Texas Hold 'em or Omaha; also known as fifth street.

rock A predictably tight player. They rarely raise unless they have the very best hand.

rounder A person who makes his or her living by playing cards.

rush A series of good cards.

sandbag Checking a good hand you intend to raise. It's a way to increase the money in the pot.

satellite A tournament with a small entry fee in which the prize is entry in a bigger tournament.

semi-bluff A bluff with outs.

set A three of a kind you get by combining the pair in your hole cards with one card on the board.

Seven-Card Stud A poker game in which players receive two down cards and one up card, followed by three up cards and a final down card. Betting rounds start after players receive the first three cards; the player with the lowest up card is first to act. In subsequent rounds, the betting is led by the player with the highest card(s).

shoot-out A tournament in which you have to eliminate every other player from your table before moving on.

short stack Having few chips left.

showdown When the remaining players in a pot turn over their hands to determine a winner.

side pot A pot created to accommodate other players who want to continue betting in a hand when a player in that hand has run out of chips.

slow play When you just check or call—weakly playing a strong hand—to keep other players in the game to increase the size of the pot.

slow roll Stalling before turning over your hand to frustrate your opponent.

steal To win a pot by bluffing.

suited Two or more cards of the same suit.

tap out To bet and lose all of your chips.

tells Behavior that gives other players information about your hand or how you will play.

three-bet The third bet made in a betting round (a reraise of a raise).

tight Style of play of someone who only plays premium hands.

tilting The general condition in which your emotions distort your ability to play your best. For example, you've lost a bundle and you're trying desperately to recoup, with a fervor that is causing you to make bad decisions. Also referred to as playing "on tilt."

top pair When one of your hole cards matches the best card on the board.

trap A player is trapped when another player with a strong hand gets the trapped player to put money in with the worst hand.

trips Any three of a kind.

turn The fourth community card dealt faceup is called the turn. In limit poker, the betting limit usually doubles on the turn.

underdog, a.k.a. **dog** The hand that is least likely to win a particular pot.

under the gun The first player to bet after the big blind.

wheel The lowest straight: A-2-3-4-5; a.k.a. bicycle.

wired A pair dealt in the first two cards—also called back-to-back.

Poker Fundamentals: Ranking of Hands

Royal Flush—The highest possible hand consists of A-K-Q-J-10, all in the same suit.

Straight Flush—Five cards of the same suit in sequence. For example, J-10-9-8-7, all in spades. If two straight flushes are competing, the one with the higher top card is the winner. An ace can be counted as either the highest or lowest card; in a straight flush like 5-4-3-2-A, the top card is the 5.

Four of a Kind (also called Quads)—Four cards of the same rank, such as four jacks.

Full House—Three cards of one rank and two cards of another rank. If two full houses are competing, to determine which is higher you look at the three of a kind. So 8-8-8-3-3 ("eights full of threes" in poker lingo) would beat 6-6-6-A-A.

Flush—Five cards of the same suit, like A-10-7-5-2 all in hearts. When comparing two flushes, the highest card determines which hand is higher. If those high cards are equal, you look at the second-highest card in each hand, and so on.

Straight—Five cards in a sequence, regardless of their suits. K-Q-J-10-9 is a straight. So is 6-5-4-3-2; but that straight would be beat by 7-6-5-4-3.

Three of a Kind—Three cards of the same rank plus any two other cards. (In poker jargon, it's called "trips.") The highest of competing trips wins.

Two Pair—A hand with two pair of equal-ranked cards. The hand with the top pair wins. So Q-Q-2-2-6 beats J-J-10-10-9. If players' top pair matches, then you look to the lower pair for the winner. If that pair matches, too, you determine the winner based on the odd card.

Pair—A hand with two cards of equal rank. The higher pair always wins. If players have the same pair, you compare the highest odd card. So J-J-A-3-2 beats J-J-K-5-4.

High Card—When players' cards form none of the above combinations, you look to the highest card to determine the winner. If the highest cards are equal, you compare the second-highest cards, and so on. So A-K-J-9-3 beats A-Q-10-8-6.

How Betting Works

When it's your turn to bet, these are your options.

Fold: This means you don't want to bet. You toss in your cards, forfeiting the right to compete for the pot and losing any money you've already bet.

Bet: If you want to bet on your hand, you place your bet on the table. In limit games (see below) you're required to bet in specified amounts.

Call: In order to stay in the pot, you're required to bet the same amount that the players before you bet.

Raise: You put in more money than the people before you. Everyone must match your raise (or reraise you even more money) in order to stay in the pot. If they do reraise you, you have to call them if you want to stay in the hand. In Limit Hold 'em, the maximum number of raises per round is usually set at three or four.

Check: This means you choose not to bet until you see if anyone else bets. You can only check until someone else bets, at which point you can fold, call, or raise.

Poker Strategy

There are two major things you should always be doing in any poker game: calculating odds and reading players.

Calculating Odds. Poker's very much about math, and if you want to win you need to be constantly running numbers in your head to determine what the odds are. Once you do the math, you minimize chance. You need to know the odds of hitting your hand. Here's a simple example: say you hold two spades, and there are two more spades on the flop. Your odds of making a flush are about 2 to 1. That means you would get that spade approximately once for every three times you play that hand; or, if you prefer percentages, about 33 percent of the time.

To calculate odds, you need to know how many outs you have—cards that can help you make your hand. In the preceding example, where your hole cards are two spades and you hit two spades on the flop, there are nine more spades in the deck. That means you have nine outs. Here's a quick way to roughly determine your odds of hitting your hand. In Texas Hold 'em you have five known cards—your two hole cards and the flop—and forty-seven unknown cards. If you have nine outs (as in the example above), you can assume you have nine good cards and thirty-eight bad cards. Divide the number of bad cards by the number of good cards and you get 4.2—so your odds of hitting your hand are 4.2 to 1. Since you have two chances to hit (on the turn and on the river), your odds become 2.1 to 1.

Then there's something called **pot odds.** Pot odds are the number of chips in the pot compared to the size of your bet. Put another way, this is the amount you can potentially win in a pot given the amount you have to bet. If there's $100 in the pot and you have to call $20, there's five times as much money in the pot as you're betting. So the pot is offering you 5-to-1 odds. If the pot has $40 in it and you have to call $20, the pot is only offering you 2-to-1 odds.

Ordinarily, if your pot odds are greater than the odds of winning your hand, you stand to make a profit and should play the hand.

In Texas Hold 'em, if you have a flush draw with two cards to come, you're about a 2-to-1 underdog (a.k.a. dog) to make the hand. So you need to make sure there's more than twice as much money in the pot as what you have to call, because you're only going to make that hand, on average, one time out of three. If you're going to make it one time out of three, your odds are a little less than 2 to 1. So you need pot odds of more than 2 to 1 to make it profitable.

Let's say you have to call $20, and you're a 2-to-1 dog. You're going to win that hand one time and lose it twice. So you'll lose $20 twice. That means when you win the hand that one time, you need to make sure that you're winning more than the $40 you're losing; you need to make sure there's more than $40 in the pot. Then, in the long run, you'll make money.

When somebody bets into you—and you have a hand like a flush draw—you know that you're a 2-to-1 dog. You look at what they bet into you. You have to consider not only that you are getting 2 to 1, but also that you'll have to call more money in the future.

So say there's $500 in the pot and a guy bets $500. The pot is $1,000. And you're the 2-to-1 dog. In that case, ordinarily you wouldn't want to call if there's exactly twice as much money as he bet—that's gambling, and you don't need to do that. You're not getting an edge either way.

Now, assume you're a 4-to-1 dog to hit a particular hand. Your opponent bets $1,000 and there's only $3,000 in the pot. But you look at his stack and see that he has $10,000. And you're pretty sure that some percentage of the time, when you make your flush, you're going to win some portion of his stack. So you actually include some potential winnings in calculating your pot odds—even though the money isn't actually in the pot right then. You can add money that you think your opponent will be adding to the pot. So if he has $10,000 in his stack you can add $2,000 into your calculations. So instead of having $3,000 in the pot you can see it as $5,000. It boosts your pot odds. So sometimes you don't need to be getting exactly the right odds for the pot right then—you can factor in future expectation. That gives you the *implied odds.*

Reading the Other Players. You're constantly assessing your opponents. Think of this challenge as a three-legged stool. Leg number one: you're making a continual psychological profile, unearthing their characters to determine what kind of person each is—a cautious person who becomes sneaky when trapped? Someone who is uncontrolled? Someone who's risk-averse?

Leg number two: you're analyzing their betting patterns. Do they make their big bets faster when they have the nuts? Or do they tend to slow play strong hands? Do they start playing irresponsibly whenever you play aggressively, or do they fold? Do they like to check-raise on drawing hands? Or do they always check-call with those hands?

Leg number three: pay attention to the tells, those unconscious gestures that are invaluable. The more you play, the better you get at picking up tells. Do they suddenly look calm? (Could be a sign that they're comfortable with their cards.) Are they blinking more than usual? (Could be a sign that they're lying.) Do they clear their throat when they bluff? By reading people, and paying close attention to their betting, you ultimately can predict with relative accuracy the hands they hold and the moves they will likely make. And then you'll do a better job of playing *them*: encouraging them to stay in a game or intimidating them into folding a hand. As Doyle Brunson put it in his landmark book *Super/System: How I Made Over $1,000,000 Playing Poker*: "Poker is a game of people. That's the most important lesson you should learn from my book."

Types of Play

Cash Games versus Tournaments. The world of poker is divided into cash games and tournaments. Tournament play is what you see on TV, but the majority of people playing poker in this country are playing cash games, also called live games.

Tournament-poker and live-game strategies are completely different, and there are some people who just can't make the transition. There are cash players who are terrible tournament players, and vice versa, mainly because they don't understand that the math is different. Plus, in a cash game, you can always reach into your pocket or go to your safe-deposit box—assuming you're not broke—and get more chips, which changes the psychology of the game. And in cash games, chips represent their real mathematical value—that is, a $5 chip is actually worth $5. In a tournament, that's not true.

In tournaments, chips are valued in relation to the prize pool, so strange mathematical things can happen to the value of your chips, the most obvious of which is that the more chips you have, the less each chip is worth. Suppose you have a stack of one hundred chips and somebody else has a stack of five. Both of you are playing for the same prize pool. So, obviously, for the person with only five chips, each chip is worth a lot more than each of your one hundred chips. The reason: you're playing for a finite number of dollars. There are certain strategies you're supposed to play when your chips aren't worth their face value.

Here's an example. If you get hold of a lot of chips in a tournament, for both psychological and mathematical reasons you should play much looser. Individually, your chips are less valuable than the chips in the pot, so you're actually getting a better price from the pot every time you play somebody who has a shorter stack.

So when you're playing in a tournament against someone with a short stack, be looser in your draws. Because each chip is worth less, you can play more hands and bet more with the hope of drawing the right cards from the flop. Your chip may say $20, and there might be $100 in the pot, but the pot is giving you better than 5-to-1 odds because you have so many chips to play.

But if it's you who has the short stack, you probably shouldn't be chasing draws. Because each of your chips is worth more, you're not actually getting a great price. Each card you pursue becomes more expensive. So it might look like the pot's offering you 2-to-1 odds on hitting a particular card, but it's not.

In cash games, stack size doesn't matter. You don't need to make any adjustments to your play because your stack is bigger or smaller than your opponents'. A dollar is a dollar, and a chip is worth its face value. And in cash games, having a huge pile of chips doesn't give you as much of a psychological edge as it does in tournaments. Depending on their resources, an opponent can make a quick exit and return with more ammo. As a result, bluffs don't work as effectively in cash games, either. When someone's running low on chips in a tournament, they should be playing more protectively. They're feeling that it's finite, and that if they lose they're going to have to walk away from the table. As their opponent, it's relatively easy for you to put psychological pressure on them.

My tournament game is vastly more aggressive than my live game. In tournaments, playing aggressively is mathematically correct—and it's psychologically correct, too. I play maybe 30 percent of my hands in tournaments, versus about 20 percent in live games.

Tournaments are much more of a high-variance situation. There's a higher degree of chance. You simply have to place in the top spots. Because of the high variance, I have a backer—my good friend Erik Seidel—who puts up 100 percent of the buy-in and gets a percent of the return. In cash games, I play my own money. When I'm playing for cash, I don't bluff as much, but I tend to play a very trappy game—that is, I sit and wait until I have the good cards and then trap my opponents.

Limit versus No-Limit. The other big distinction is limit versus no-limit. In limit games, you have to bet or raise in fixed increments. At a $2-$4 limit table, the small blind is $1 and the big blind is $2. You're limited to betting in $2 increments during the first two bets and in $4 increments during the second two bets. You're also limited to four raises.

What that ultimately means is that there are restrictions not only on the size of pot you can win but also on your strategic options. In no-limit, you can make a huge bet if you want to discourage an opponent from calling. You can push your chips all-in when you feel you have an unbeatable hand, or when you see an opportunity to bluff an opponent, or when you're low on chips and have nothing to lose. You push your chips into the center of the table, forcing your opponent to either call or fold. For its upside potential and strategic complexity, I prefer no-limit. It's more demanding than limit, but also more exciting.

Limit is a slower game, with far fewer openings for aggressive players like me. In no-limit, anything can happen—and you can win a lot more money in a shorter amount of time.

I love the way no-limit is described by Matt Damon's character in the movie *Rounders*:

> *No-limit. There's no other game in which fortunes can change so much from hand to hand. A brilliant player can get a strong hand cracked, go "on tilt" and lose his mind along with every single chip in front of him. This is why the World Series of Poker is decided over a no-limit Hold 'em table. Some people, pros even, won't play no-limit. They can't handle the swings.*

The Rules of Texas Hold 'em

The version of poker that has conquered television, the Internet, college dorms, and millions of kitchen tables over the last couple of years is Texas Hold 'em. The game's popularity stems from its deceptive simplicity; its astoundingly easy-to-learn rules mask its chesslike complexity. Also, the game's format allows it to be easily televised and widely understood.

The object is to win the pot by making the best possible five-card hand, using one or both or neither of your two face-down cards (hole cards) and any of the five faceup cards (the board) that are laid out in the center of the table. Or you can win the pot by bluffing your opponents into folding their hands because they *think* you have the best possible hand.

Each player is dealt two cards facedown. There is a round of betting. Then three cards (the flop) are dealt faceup in the center of the table. These are the community cards shared by all the players. After the flop, there is another round of betting. The dealer then deals another community card (the turn card—a.k.a. fourth street). There's another round of betting. Then the dealer turns a final community card (the river—a.k.a. fifth street). There is a final betting round, followed by a showdown. In limit games, there is a fixed amount that you can bet. In $5-$10 games, you bet $5 in the first two betting rounds (pre-flop and after the flop), and $10 in the next two (after the turn and after the river).

Betting starts with the person to the left of the dealer and moves clockwise around the table. Betting order is important, and players in late betting positions—the last ones to bet—have the advantage of knowing what their opponents have done. In most home games, everybody gets to become the dealer, with the job moving clockwise by one player after each hand. In cases where a single person is dealing—such as in tournaments or in casino games—a little disk known as the button is placed in front of the person who would be the dealer if the deal rotated clockwise to each successive player after each hand.

The first bet actually occurs before the cards are dealt. To get the action started, the person to the dealer's (or button's) immediate left must post a predetermined amount known as the "small blind" (say, $5). The person to his immediate left must post twice that amount, known as the "big blind" ($10). This is intended to get the action started. When the full round of betting reaches players in the blinds, they must increase their bets from their blind bet to the current bet. (They can also raise or fold.)

In No-Limit Hold 'em, if you don't have enough chips to call an opponent's bet, you can call "all-in" for all your remaining chips. If no one else is in the pot, your opponent takes back his excess chips, and the hand is played to conclusion without additional betting. If other players remain, a side pot may be created for those players.

Rules of Omaha Hi-Lo Split

Omaha Hi-Lo Split (also referred to as Omaha 8-or-Better) is a four-card version of Texas Hold 'em. You're dealt four hole cards instead of two.

In both games, there are five community cards. In Texas Hold 'em, you can use any combination of the seven cards to make the best five-card hand. In Omaha, you can't use just any combination of the nine cards: you must use exactly two from your hole cards and three from the board. The goal is to get both the best five-card high hand and the best five-card low hand. You're allowed to use different hole cards in making your low hand than you use in making your high hand.

As with Texas Hold 'em, there are four rounds of betting—before the flop, before the turn, before the river, and after the river—followed by a showdown.

A qualifying low hand in Omaha is made with five cards that are all 8 or lower, with an ace counting as the lowest. No pairs can exist in a low hand, but you can have a straight and/or a flush. The lowest possible hand is A-2-3-4-5. The highest qualifying low hand is 4-5-6-7-8. So if the board comes J-J-8-7-6, the best possible low would be 8-7-6-2-A. If you had in your hand a deuce and an ace, you'd have the nut low. If you had an ace and a 3 in your hand, you would use them for 8-7-6-3-A.

While Texas Hold 'em is a game with one winner per hand, in Omaha the pot gets split. But sometimes it goes to one player, which is called "scooping."

The player with the best high hand wins half the pot, and the player with the best low hand wins the other half. If there is no qualifying low hand, the player with the best high hand scoops the entire pot. You also get to scoop if you have both the best high and low hands. In Omaha, it's extremely important to scoop the pot. That's where most of your edge comes from—getting the whole pot instead of getting half of it.

The idea in Omaha is that, when possible, you want to be playing very strong low holdings, so that you have the best possible low made already—which means you have half the pot locked up. And then you can make high sort of accidentally.

This is called free rolling. Good players want to be free rolling because it's nice to have your equity locked up. You get to say, "Okay, half this pot is mine. Let's see if I can get the other half from you." In Omaha, it's important to avoid playing middle cards, hands like 9-8-7-6.

The very best hand you can have in Omaha 8-or-Better is A-A-2-3, double suited. That way you have the A-2, A-3, and 2-3 for the low side. And you have two aces for the high side. You have two nut flush draws with your A-2 suited and A-3 suited. It's an extremely powerful hand because you have lots of high possibilities and lots of low possibilities.

Another really great hand is A-K-2-3, with two suits. In this hand you have all the low possibilities with the A-2-3, but then you also have the A-K on the high side with an ace-high flush draw and a king-high flush draw.

As I mentioned, there's another way to scoop, which is merely to make high and no low. So another type of really powerful hand is one that has all high potential, a hand like K-K-Q-J double suited. When you hit that hand, there are usually not going to be any low possibilities on the board. Say that's your hand and the board comes K-10-10. You need to have three low cards on the board to qualify a low hand. But in this case, there are no low cards. With no possible lows, you will scoop the pot with your high hand ("kings full of tens").

Omaha is not more complex than Texas Hold 'em—it just feels that way. One of the biggest differences is that the math is not as transparent. As a result, people tend to make bigger errors in Omaha. But once you understand the math, it's not particularly more complicated, it's just that the issue of the pot being split changes the odds of the game drastically. Omaha is a very mathematical game, so it suits my strength, which is basically math. What I find fascinating about Hold 'em is that it's a game that—more than any other—reveals its complexities the more you play it.

People to Watch

Finally, you'll need a playlist to follow my tournament action, so I've compiled an alphabetized Who's Who of many of the players mentioned in this book.

Eli Balas is an Israeli man in his fifties, a solid player who does particularly well in tournaments—he's won three World Series of Poker bracelets. A former diamond merchant, he's a regular at the Bellagio. I lost a heartbreaking hand to him when we were heads-up at the final table of the 1999 World Series of Poker $5,000 Limit Hold 'em event.

Todd Bleak is six feet three and sports a Wyatt Earp mustache. The forty-six-year-old father of five grew up in the Las Vegas area and has been playing poker since he was eighteen. He now lives in Downey, California, where he trains poker dealers at the Bicycle Casino. He made it to the final table of the 2004 World Series of Poker $2,000 Buy-In Omaha Hi-Lo Split.

Ray Bonavida plays regularly at the Commerce Casino in Los Angeles and hasn't had a lot of high-level tournament experience, although he was strong enough to make it to the final table of the $2,000 Buy-In Omaha Hi-Lo Split with me. The $30,140 he earned in that tournament comprised the bulk of his tournament winnings—and I hope it's a harbinger of winnings to come; before that he had won less than $4,000 in tournaments. He's a good-looking, goateed man in his early thirties who sports sunglasses and a sort of European flair.

Boston is the nickname of Alan Dvorkis, although he's been known by a bunch of names over the years. He formerly had a head full of red hair and was known universally as "Boston Red." Now he's bald, so he's just plain Boston. He also has been referred to as Alan Boston. Because he's had so many names—and so many final-table appearances—his tournament cash wins have to be tallied up with three different names. He's an old friend of my brother's, and we've been friends ourselves for about ten years. He's one of the greatest college basketball handicappers of all time. He was one of three professional gamblers tracked by author Chad Millman for an entire college basketball season for the book *The Odds.* He owns a racehorse named Unserveabull. Boston is something of a stud specialist and an excellent Omaha player. We started out together at the same table of the $2,000 Omaha Hi-Lo Split. He ended up in twenty-seventh place—which is just in the money.

Humberto Brenes is one of a crew of great players from Costa Rica. Warm and friendly, he owns a string of businesses in his native country, including a TV station, a construction company, and restaurants. He holds a degree in industrial engineering. He was especially kind to me when he saw how devastated I was about knocking out my brother in the final event of the 1994 World Series of Poker.

Todd Brunson is a heavyset guy with a large mullet he always wears in a ponytail. He rivals his famous dad, Doyle, in size. He's one of the best heads-up Hold 'em players in the world, and he's one of the people who play the famous Texas billionaire (who's a fish, so I don't want to name him). Todd and my brother are the most successful against that guy. Todd and Howard have played these heads-up $50,000 and $100,000 games at the Bellagio, where they play off in a corner and it's just them and this billionaire, who really just wants to play against the best in the world. Todd crushes him a lot. He applies his aggressions in very good spots. He's a good reader and he's able to change to adapt to his opponent's style of play, which is really important.

My brother has that trait, too. Howard's more analytical and measured. Todd is more instinctual. But Todd is a very smart guy. He's made a lot of money in the stock market and on investments, and he's won a lot of tournaments. He's won a total of nearly $300,000 in tournaments, and landed at the final table of the $2,000 Omaha Hi-Lo event with me at the 2004 WSOP.

Doyle "Texas Dolly" Brunson is an inspiration to everyone who's played against him. At age seventy-one, he's still at the top of his game—and still incredibly funny. A cancer survivor, he's won two World Series of Poker Championship events, and over the years has accumulated nine WSOP bracelets. Last year he outlasted 666 opponents to win the Legends of Poker tournament. We both competed at the World Series of Poker Tournament of Champions. The West Texas son had been drafted by the NBA's Minneapolis Lakers (later the LA Lakers), but a knee injury sent his career elsewhere; he sold adding machines for a few weeks before deciding there was more promise in poker. He was one of the original road gamblers, and he shares stories about the days when players literally had to have a gun on them while playing poker—it was that fraught with danger. His famous book *Super/System* is incomparable. Since its publication in the 1970s, it has helped generations of poker players to improve their games.

Johnny Chan is scary good. One of the best poker players who has ever played the game, he has been intimidating opponents at the table for three decades. It's his mere presence that's intimidating—just because he's such a solid player. He has a penchant for silk Versace shirts in loud patterns—you see him on TV and you get up to adjust your set. He won back-to-back World Series of Poker Championship events in 1987 and 1988, and came in second to Phil Hellmuth in 1989. In the movie *Rounders*, there's a famous scene of him beating my friend Erik at the final table—a fact that I never let Erik forget. Ask anyone in poker—they'll tell you that Johnny Chan has the best eyes. He was at the table with me at the World Series of Poker Tournament of Champions.

T. J. Cloutier is an imposing physical presence, all six feet five inches and 290 pounds of him. He's a former linebacker and tight end in the Canadian Football League, and a former derrick man on an oil rig. When I first started playing in Las Vegas in the mid-1990s, he was already a champ and always really nice to me—always open when I asked about hands. I remember folding a K-Q to a reraise, and I asked him afterward if that was the kind of hand he would have folded. He said, "Absolutely." Outside of my brother, he was one of the players I learned the most from. We faced each other at the World Series of Poker Tournament of Champions.

Artie Cobb is one of the greatest Stud players of all time. He's been playing professionally since the 1970s and is one of the sweetest people I know. He's won more than $1 million at World Series of Poker events. In 1991 he came in first place in the WSOP $1,500 Seven-Card Stud event. He also came in first in the 1998 WSOP $2,500 Seven-Card Stud event. We found ourselves at the same table at the $2,000 Omaha Hi-Lo Split event.

Allen Cunningham is a young phenom—he's twenty-six years old—who arrived on the scene in 2000. He started playing at Indian casinos when he was eighteen and dropped out of UCLA, where he was pursuing a degree in engineering, to play poker full-time. He won the $5,000 Seven-Card Stud Tournament of the 2001 WSOP, the $5,000 No-Limit Deuce-to-Seven Tournament of the 2002 WSOP, and the $1,500 No-Limit Hold 'em Tournament of the 2005 WSOP. I faced him at an early table of the $2,500 Limit Hold 'em Tournament at the Bellagio.

Nani Dollison had one amazing year (2001) when she won more than $440,000 at the World Series of Poker, but I haven't seen her around much since then. She's a native of Korea and a former card dealer in Tunica, Mississippi. I was the leading money winner among women at the World Series of Poker until 2001, when she won the opening Limit Hold 'em event, which attracted six hundred players—a number that would have been unheard of only a few years earlier.

Antonio "the Magician" Esfandiari is a really cool guy. He emigrated to the United States from Iran at the age of eight and barely spoke English. By the time he turned eighteen he had become an expert magician who performed regularly at corporate events. Three years later he realized he could make more money playing poker. At the age of twenty-five he became the youngest player to win a World Poker Tour event—the 2004 LA Poker Classic at the Commerce—which earned him more than $1.4 million. He followed that up by winning his first bracelet at the WSOP the day after I played in the $2,000 Omaha Hi-Lo Split. We competed at the same table at the $2,500 Limit Hold 'em event at the Bellagio.

Chris "Jesus" Ferguson is a great friend of mine and one of the most easily recognizable players in the game. You see him everywhere, this soft-spoken, even-natured Jesus look-alike, with his thin frame, his flowing brown hair, his red boots, and his omnipresent black Stetson ringed with a silver band. It's a hat that rests on a head that has earned a Ph.D. in artificial intelligence from UCLA. He's a math guy whose biggest moment occurred at the championship event of the 2000 World Series of Poker, when he went heads-up with T. J. Cloutier to win first place and $2.5 million. He's so far won five WSOP bracelets. We ended up at the same table during the $2,000 Omaha Hi-Lo event.

Perry Friedman is a friend I've known for years. I didn't know him when he was a renowned prankster at Stanford, didn't know him when he slipped into a navy-blue velvet evening gown to pose as Frieda Friedman so he and other cross-dressers-for-a-day poker buddies could play in a ladies-only poker tournament at San Jose's Bay 101 Club. I wasn't there when he wrote his first computer program for the game Roshambo (rock, paper, scissors), or when he won the Omaha Hi-Lo Tournament in the 2002 World Series of Poker, walking off with $176,000. He's married to my friend Kim, whom he met on the Internet. Perry and I have ingested many a green apple (Midori, Stoli, Sweet & Sour) together. We started at the same table at the 2004 Omaha Hi-Lo event. Fortunately, he didn't have to dress in drag for that one.

Ron Graham is a fifty-three-year-old professional poker player from Tacoma, Washington, who lives in Las Vegas. He's something of a mystery man among many of the pros I know. He shows up for tournaments, but doesn't seem to hang around with other pros—or at least not with ones I'm familiar with. He's a nice guy. Quiet. Perhaps even a bit shy. My friend Erik busted him out of the 1988 World Series of Poker Championship event. Ron came in third. Erik came in second. Two years earlier Ron had won a bracelet in the WSOP $5,000 Deuce-to-

Seven Draw event. He's on the short side, with thin, blond hair. He was possibly the only person at the final table of the 2004 WSOP $2,000 Omaha Hi-Lo Split who wasn't cracking jokes.

Gus Hansen, also known as the Great Dane, has a shorn head and abs that would rival those of a professional athlete. Gus is a charming and talkative player who was a famous backgammon player in Europe before taking up poker.

Jennifer Harman is a tiny five feet two and weighs 100 pounds soaking wet. She's blonde and comes from the Italian family that owned the track concessions in Reno-Sparks and Carson City. She played poker in her dad's home games and snuck into casinos when she was sixteen. A homecoming queen, she studied biology at the University of Nevada and started her working life as a cocktail waitress in poker rooms. Now she's the only woman who plays in the highest cash games in the world—since I moved away from Las Vegas. She's battled kidney problems in recent years and has undergone two kidney transplants.

Phil Hellmuth discovered poker at the University of Wisconsin and in 1989, at age twenty-four, became the youngest person ever to win the Final Event of the World Series of Poker. He's won nine World Series bracelets. Phil doesn't know this but he's the quintessential white-guy dancer. He loves dancing—and he's really awful. Still, I hang out with him all the time because he has a terrific heart and he's incredibly loyal to his friends. He's the one who really pushed ultimatebet.com to hire me and I'm eternally grateful, because it's been a great opportunity and I love working with the site. Go out with Phil and you have to order Dom Perignon. Either that or sweet German wine. Phil's a likeable nerd, not the least bit hip to popular culture. I'd really hate to know what's on his iPod. Phil's known as the Poker Brat because while he has a very good heart he doesn't quite know how to behave at the table.

Richard "the Shadow" Hoffmaster has an awesome sense of humor. A retired PGA golfer, he owns a small golf course and restaurant in Missoula, Montana. Now sixty years old, he learned poker from his mother when he was seven and supported himself at the University of Wisconsin by playing poker. He didn't play the game for three decades (1967 to 1997), and only started participating in big tournaments in the past four years. Of the five World Series of Poker events he's entered, he's made two final tables—including the $2,000 Omaha Hi-Lo event. He still looks like he's ready to tee off, with his white visor cap, his cashmere crewneck sweaters, his Levi's Dockers. He's five feet eight, weighs 180 pounds, and has slicked-back brown hair and a mustache.

Phil Ivey burst on the scene at the age of twenty-three and was one of a group of young guys who changed the way poker is played today; he's extremely aggressive and plays lots of hands. Most winning players start out with only the best hands, but Phil is willing to start out with the worst hands. Because he's such a good reader of players, it's to his advantage to play as many hands as possible. It takes a particular genius to walk the line between throwing your money away by playing too many hands and crushing your opponents by using the same strategy. He appears to all the world as a quiet guy, but he is incredibly sarcastic and dead-on in his observations. African-American and astonishingly good-looking, he's a master of hip-hop style who always wears big basketball jerseys. Phil became a dominant force in the biggest cash games in the world in his twenties—games that had been dominated by people in their thirties and forties, with far more experience. That shows what a genius he is.

Howard "the Professor" Lederer (I call him "Bub") is the world's best older brother. Also the wisest. Without him I'd still be playing at the Crystal Lounge in Billings, Montana. Howard has won two World Series of Poker bracelets. Before 2004 he was the youngest player to make it to the WSOP Championship event main table, placing fifth in 1987, when he was twenty-four years old. His cool, calculated, analytical style of play has earned him his nickname. He's also recognized for his killer stare. Behind that stare exists a vegetarian Grateful Dead and hip-hop fan whose quick mathematical mind has led Wall Street firms to try to lure him from his true passions: poker and sports betting. Among players and fans alike, he's phenomenally well respected, and not just by his little sis.

Toto (real name: Alfredo) Leonidas is a diminutive, quiet, Philippines-born player who was almost late for the start of the final table of the $1,500 Seven-Card Stud event in the 2003 World Series because he spent much of the morning—it was

Good Friday—in church. His religious experience paid off for him. He won that event. We faced each other early in the $2,000 Omaha Hi-Lo event.

Kathy Liebert left the corporate life and her job as a Dun & Bradstreet executive to play professional poker. Blonde-haired and friendly, she started out playing in Colorado in 1991 and has since won nearly $2 million in tournaments, including a bracelet for the $1,500 Limit Hold 'em Shoot-out at the 2004 World Series of Poker. She's a good player; not very gregarious.

James McManus made a splash with his bestselling book *Positively Fifth Street*, about his experiences in the 2000 World Series of Poker, where he came in fourth in the Championship event. I remember being so miserable when I played that year. I was one month away from giving birth to Lucy, and I didn't want to talk to *anybody.* I was uncomfortable and not feeling friendly. He made many attempts to interview me, but in my hormonal state I wasn't that helpful to him. My inaccessibility resulted in a not always positive portrayal in his book; needless to say, I've since learned to be helpful to reporters. Buoyed by his success at the WSOP, McManus has become a regular on the tournament circuit. He's on the short side, balding, and wears glasses.

Don McNamara is a Bay Area businessman who has been playing in poker tournaments for three years. His winnings total

$35,610, including the $21,520 he won in the 2004 WSOP $2,000 Omaha Hi-Lo Split, where we played together at the final table. Don is forty years old and has an MBA in finance. He's six feet tall, sports curly brown hair and a beard, and wears wire-frame glasses.

Daniel Negreanu is a talkative, slight-built Canadian who dyes the tips of his hair and wears multiple earrings. His style of dress alternates from hockey jerseys to spiffy clothes. He's been very successful and has his own unusual style of play—he plays a lot of hands and talks constantly while he plays. Both traits tend to have the effect of confusing his opponents. Outside of Greg Raymer, who won the World Series of Poker Championship event, Daniel was the biggest money winner in tournament poker in 2004. At the 2004 WSOP, he won the Toyota Player of the Year award.

Men "the Master" Nguyen fled Vietnam in a boat in 1977 at the age of twenty-three and was working as a machinist in Los Angeles when he discovered poker during a $30 junket to Vegas in 1984. He played every weekend for a year before entering his first tournament. By 1996 he took fourth place in the World Series of Poker Championship event, and a year later was named *Card Player* magazine's Player of the Year. He's been at hundreds of final tables—twenty of them at World Series events. You can pick him out at any table. He's the one with a bottle of Corona grafted onto his hand. He drinks it because he says it relaxes him and helps him focus. He's been known to say he can drink ten to fifteen of them without getting drunk.

Five feet four inches tall and 135 pounds, Men also has a few other trademarks. A lemon-colored Buddha-bead bracelet. A massive pinky ring. Monogrammed pants. And, I'm told, a tattoo on his right thigh bearing the name of the island in Malaysia where he spent six months in a refugee camp. A World Series of Poker Omaha event is among the six WSOP events he has won in his career. We started at the same table in the 2004 WSOP $2,000 Omaha Hi-Lo event.

Greg Raymer you can recognize, if you've watched poker on TV, by his silly round glasses. Like a lot of poker players, Greg is jovial, sweet, and a little nerdy. (A lot of people probably imagine poker pros to be slick, dark, and nefarious.) I met Greg when we played together at the 2004 World Series of Poker Tournament of Champions, a few months after he won the WSOP Championship event. After meeting him I was happy that he was one of the main representatives of poker; he is a classy guy. I had played a hand against him in the TOC and folded a pair of tens, which knocked me down to $150,000 because I put Greg on aces or kings. As the tournament went on, I had second thoughts about that hand. When Greg was eventually knocked out of the tournament, he graciously shook my hand and whispered, "I had kings on that hand," putting my mind at ease. He didn't have to do that.

Chip Reese is probably the best poker player to have ever walked the earth. He's amiable, likable, and incredibly smart. After graduating from Dartmouth thirty years ago, he stopped in Vegas, where he planned to spend the summer, on his way to grad school at Stanford. He had $400 in his pocket. By the end of the summer he had turned that into $100,000. Needless to say, he never made it to Stanford. Instead he has become a legend in cash games—he's probably won more in poker cash games than anyone else—as well as a great tournament player. He's one of the few living members of the Poker Hall of Fame.

Matt Savage is one of the hardest workers in poker. He's a sprite. A former dealer, he's morphed into one of the best and most respected tournament directors in the game. You can instantly identify him by his trademark Nehru jacket; it's a look that belies his amiable, boyish charm.

Erik Seidel—what can I say about Erik? I don't think there's a more decent, honest individual on the face of the earth—in addition to being one of the world's best no-limit players. He's been a true friend to me for more than a decade. His wisdom and patience and kindness and intellect are legendary, as is his sense of humor, which most people don't actually consider a sense of humor because it is so mercilessly droll. He could be the poker world's Johnny Carson. The former Wall Street bond trader has won seven World Series of Poker bracelets. I'm the first to admit that poker is full of all sorts of questionable characters. But then there's Erik, who is rock-solid. He's six feet six, but it's not his height that makes him stand out at the table—it's that he's recognized from a famous movie scene in *Rounders*: a younger version of himself losing to Johnny Chan. When something aggravating, momentous, funny, or sad happens in my life, he's one of the first people I call.

Barry Shulman is the owner and publisher of *Card Player* magazine. Gray-haired, and with a bit of a paunch, Shulman earned an accounting degree from the University of Washington and spent twenty-five years developing real estate in the Seattle area before retiring to Las Vegas in the 1990s. He started getting into poker and saw the business potential in a magazine devoted to the game. So he invested his nest egg to buy and greatly expand *Card Player*, which at the time was little more than a casino handout. He launched it onto newsstands at the end of 2003, just as poker was taking off. Today it's something of a must-read for fans and players alike. We competed at the 2004 World Series of Poker $2,000 Omaha Hi-Lo event—where he was catching far better cards than I was getting.

Max Stern has been playing tournament poker for a long time. He's a grandfather, and a retired pediatrician, who lives for half the year in Costa Rica, where he practiced medicine. He always wears the championship poker jacket. He's won a couple of World Series of Poker bracelets and always has one of them on. He's short and sports a mustache. Some folks call him "Doctor Max." We both landed at the final table of the 2004 World Series of Poker $2,000 Omaha Hi-Lo event.

Robert Williamson III is a gregarious Texan who has a generous soul and a talent for getting everyone around him to join the party. I met him at a little tournament at the Orleans during a time when I was the object of a smear campaign and quickly losing self-confidence. I knew him peripherally, but he went out of his way to make sure that I knew he supported me. And for that I'll always be grateful. We eventually became the best of friends. He and his clan are now part of my extended family.

Paul Wolfe is a short guy from Philly—now living in Florida—who, given the chance, will talk your ear off. He's the only one who can beat me at that game, and by a long shot. What you get for having your ears fall off is a loyal, devoted friend. He's a man of great integrity and a model father. He grew up in a family with eight brothers and sisters and has a strong middle-class work ethic. He's fun to go out with, partly because he's got a boyish vibe. Paul always wears a turned-around baseball cap.

ACKNOWLEDGMENTS

Before embarking on this book I never imagined how much of a group effort it would become. What's that African saying about raising a child—"it takes a village"? My own village got started with my sister Katy Lederer, who came up with the idea of doing an autobiographical book in the first place and who introduced me to my literary agent, Betsy Lerner. Betsy became an enthusiastic supporter, tirelessly working to make this book happen. She got Laureen Rowland, editor and founder of Hudson Street Press, an imprint of Penguin Group, excited about the project. Laureen was so convinced of the need to tell my story—even before I won a major tournament—she spent nine months slaving to get this book off the ground. She believed in me, and for that I owe her my heartfelt appreciation.

Betsy introduced me to my coauthor, David Diamond, who is just a truly awesome guy. Relentless in pursuit of detail, he crisscrossed the country, from Concord to San Diego to Philadelphia to Portland and, on about a dozen occasions, to Las Vegas. David shaped the book, got me focused and jazzed up during red-eye flights and countless late-night parties, was an expert at extracting memories—both pleasant and painful—and at crafting the chapters. I couldn't have asked for a more competent, energetic, or wise collaborator. (Although I've seen him play cards and have this to report: He should stick to writing.)

I also enjoyed getting to know his charming wife, Tia, and talented daughter, Kaley.

David's agent Kris Dahl at ICM provided useful feedback that is reflected on these pages, and Brant Janeway, the Penguin marketing genius—a poker player himself—was a font of great ideas. I'd like to thank a few other members of the Penguin team who put their stamp on this book. Melissa Jacoby designed the terrific jacket. Norina Frabotta shepherded the manuscript through production, Dana Rosen gave us her legal advice, Eve Kirch assembled the photo section, and Danielle Friedman provided editorial support. That was the New York crew. In Sausalito, Susan Dupuis could be counted on to transcribe our tapes in record time—and with minimal advance warning. Thank you. Thank you. Thank you. Thank you. Thank you.

I am fortunate to have so many friends whose support and encouragement were critical to me during the year it took to produce this book. My friends and colleagues at UltimateBet have made my poker journey even more interesting. It is a joy to work with people you also love dearly. Pamela Bruce was my original agent at ICM. Brandi Hummel is the nanny who is wonderful with my kids. My agent Michael Kernan, my managers Glen Clarkson and Cat Josell, and my business manager Kimberly Quackenbush all have kept my life sane.

I want to thank the community of poker players, who are

the best people on earth. I gush over many of them in these pages, but there are a few who deserve more gushing. Erik Seidel has been one of my best friends for over a decade and has always supported me in both my personal and poker life. His dry sense of humor is always welcome in my day, and I hold him up as a standard for graciousness and integrity. Robert Williamson III, who I love as a member of my family, has been a great friend as well. It is wonderful to have people in your life who you know would go to the mat for you.

Finally, I have the world's best family to thank, starting with my father, Richard Lederer, and my mother, Deedy. Their support and love allowed their children to make their way in the world with confidence that we could conquer anything we tried. Their faith in us has never wavered. Where most parents would have freaked out at the prospect of their children becoming professional poker players, my parents have always supported us, knowing it made us happy—which was all that mattered to them. Their eccentric good humor has made me the person I am today, and I am so thankful to them for the way I was raised. I'm also thankful for Mom's boyfriend Dale Parry and Dad's wife Simone Van Egeren. They're both terific—and were phenomenally helpful in gathering the photos for this book.

And my brother, Howard Lederer. Without Howard I would never have become a poker player and certainly not the quality of player I have become. He believed in my becoming a top player even when I was just playing small games in Billings, Montana. When he told me after my first World Series of Poker tournament that he thought I would become the leading female money winner at the WSOP, I thought he was crazy. His belief in me has kept me going. I could not ask for a more loyal, loving, wonderful brother.

But winning all the poker tournaments in the world would mean nothing compared to the love and happiness I share with my children, Maud, Leo, Lucy, and Nelly. No matter what cards I'm dealt at the poker table, I know I've been delivered the most winning hand when it comes to my kids. For that I feel lucky—and blessed. I hold each of you in my heart every day of my life.

ABOUT THE AUTHOR

Annie Duke is one of the world's best poker players. In 2004, she won $2 million in the World Series of Poker Tournament of Champions, as well as her first World Series of Poker gold bracelet, making her the only woman ever to win two major tournaments in one year.

While Annie grew up in a card-playing family (her brother, Howard Lederer, is also a top-ranked poker pro and a regular on the World Poker Tour and ESPN broadcasts), young Annie was devoted to a career in academia when she developed a panic disorder just prior to completing work for her Ph.D. at the University of Pennsylvania. Suddenly terrified of a life in academia, she married a friend—a man she had never dated—and fled to Columbus, Montana (population: 1,500). When they were unable to make their $125-a-month mortgage payments, Annie drove the fifty-one frontier miles to the Crystal Lounge in Billings, where she began to hone her skills at the poker table, and quickly started to win. Soon after, she and her new husband upped the ante and moved to Las Vegas so that she could play in bigger, higher-stakes tournaments; in the meantime, she gave birth to four children, currently between the ages of three and ten.

Annie has appeared on *Good Morning America* and the *Late Show with David Letterman*; she has also been featured in *People*, the *Los Angeles Times*, *Maxim*, *Ladies' Home Journal*, and CBS news online, as well as several popular poker publications and Web sites. In addition to playing in tournaments, Annie consults and leads online workshops for ultimatebet.com. She and her children live in Portland, Oregon.